VISUAL QUICKSTART GUIDE

NETSCAPE 3

FOR WINDOWS

Elizabeth Castro

Visual QuickStart Guide
Netscape 3 for Windows
Elizabeth Castro

Peachpit Press
2414 Sixth Street
Berkeley, CA 94710
(510) 548-4393
(510) 548-5991 (fax)

Find us on the World Wide Web at: http://www.peachpit.com

Peachpit Press is a division of Addison Wesley Longman

ISBN: 0-201-69409-3

0 9 8 7 6 5 4 3 2 1

Printed in the United States of America

For Becky and Jenny who taught me my multiplication tables,
my Uncle Myron Pollyea who taught me exponential powers,
and Stephen Ucich, my first (and only) computer teacher.

Special thanks to:

Kaethin Prizer, Kate Reber, and **Nolan Hester** at Peachpit Press for their great suggestions and corrections, and for their calm replies to frantic, last minute questions.

The folks who frequent the **netscape.navigator** newsgroup and who seem to know all the answers.

Andreu, for everything else.

Table of Contents

Table of contents

Introduction

The beauty—and the peril—of the World Wide Web is that everyone can publish their own information quickly and easily. As such, the Web is the fastest growing area in the computer world today. Each month thousands of new pages are added, by huge companies and private citizens alike.

Some pages are serious collections of commercial information. Others are personal accounts of travels, history, and life itself. Still others attempt to fill the void that the paper publishing industry is unable to answer. Perhaps the nicest thing about the Web is that there are pages about everything, from cancer research to bowling, from solar panel design to hot new bands.

What is the Web, really?

The Internet is a huge collection of computers that are connected to each other. Some computers are connected to the Internet through a telephone and modem (and are thus only *on* the Internet when they are connected). Other computers are permanently connected (generally, universities and large companies fall into this category).

There are different ways of communicating over the Internet, called *protocols*. E-mail is the most common protocol, but you may have heard of FTP, Gopher, Usenet, and HTTP, as well. This last protocol, HTTP, is the method computers use to connect to each other and view Web pages.

What is a Web page?

A Web page is nothing more than a text document with special tags. These tags add formatting, images, and hypertext links to the page. But because a Web page is a text document, in ASCII format, it can be opened on virtually any platform, from Macintosh to Windows, and including everything in between.

Although you could open a Web page with a text editor, the special tags are not interpreted unless you open the page with a browser. There are many different kinds of browsers, with different versions of each for each kind of computer platform.

Netscape Navigator

Netscape Navigator is the most popular browser, used by some 70% of the people on the World Wide Web. Commonly known as Netscape (but *not* Navigator), it combines a first-class browser with news and mail capabilities.

A special edition of the software, called Netscape Navigator Gold (or Netscape Gold, for short), also gives you the ability to create your own Web pages without having to know much about HTML.

This book is divided into four principal sections: browsing (for viewing the Web), mail (for e-mail), news (for reading newsgroups), and editing (for creating Web pages with Netscape Gold).

The illustrations in the first three sections of this book were taken with Netscape. Only the editing section shows Netscape Gold. However, you can use Netscape Gold to do everything the "plain" version does, and more.

What's new in version 3

Although Netscape 3 is certainly an improvement over version 2, it may not quite warrant a full number increase. The changes are mostly cosmetic and one gets the feeling the decision to call it version 3 was made in the marketing department and not by the software engineers. Nevertheless, this book has been completely updated to take into account all these changes, both minor and major.

Browser changes

- A number of plug-ins are included with Netscape 3 that give it the capacity to display audio, video, and other multimedia files *(see page 41)*.

- Navigating frames is much easier now that the Back and Forward commands affect individual frames and not just whole pages *(see page 39)*.

- QuickTime movies are easier to incorporate within Web pages and can be viewed directly with Netscape.

- Netscape 3 supports a variety of new HTML tags, like the FRAMEBORDER attribute for frames, the MULTICOL tag for creating multiple columns, the SPACER tag for adjusting white space on a page, the S tag as an abbreviated STRIKE tag, the FACE attribute for fonts lets the designer prefer individual fonts for viewing and the BGCOLOR tag for tables allows individual colors for cells, rows or columns.

- There are now several new international versions, including Danish, Dutch, French, German, Italian, Japanese, Korean, Brazilian Portuguese, Spanish, and Swedish.

Mail and News changes

- The new Wrap Long Lines option in the Message Composition window ensures that messages are not sent with excessively long lines of text (see page 116).

- The Wrap Long Lines option in the Mail and News window improves the appearance of (without materially changing) incoming messages with excessively long lines (see page 109).

- The panes of both the Mail and News windows can be divided horizontally as well as vertically, or stacked, as desired (see page 91).

- The Show Headers submenu offers three options for displaying information about incoming and outgoing messages and postings (see page 113).

Editor changes (Netscape Gold only)

- You can have Netscape save your document automatically every few minutes (see page 171).

- You can apply the Underlined format to text (see page 176).

- You can create tables (see page 214).

- You can display tables as a list in order to speed up work on other sections of the page (see page 174).

- You can display paragraph marks (see page 174).

- The Page Wizard has been improved and made easier to use, although it's still pretty slow (see page 166).

What's new in version 3

Part I:
Netscape Navigator

Web surfing, mail, and news

The Web Browser

Figure 1.1 *Choose New Web Browser in the File menu to open a new browser.*

Figure 1.2 *A fresh browser opens. The contents of the Location field (and of the page itself) depend on the settings you've entered in the Appearance tab of the General Preferences dialog box.*

Netscape has three types of principal windows: the Mail window, the News window, and Web browsers (sometimes called *browser windows*). You use browsers to view the pages available on the World Wide Web and to connect to FTP and Gopher sites.

Opening or closing a browser

You may open as many browsers as your computer's memory will permit in order to display several different pages at once. This is often useful if you want to follow a link on one page without losing track of the original source page.

To open a browser:

Choose New Web Browser in the File menu **(Figure 1.1)**.

To close a browser:

Choose Close in the File menu or click the browser's close box.

✔ Tips

- Netscape automatically opens a new browser upon launch. You can have it display a specific page of your choosing, including a blank page, *(see page 17)*, or skip the browser altogether and begin with the Mail or News windows *(see page 246)*.

- If a browser is already open when you open a second one, the first page opened with the first browser is displayed again in the new one.

Opening or closing a browser

The parts of the browser

Each browser has a number of elements that help you view the pages on the World Wide Web.

The page's title, as defined by the page's author, appears in Netscape's title bar.

The Edit button only appears in Netscape Gold.

Menu bar

Minimize
Whole Window
Close

Location field. To use it, see page 26. To hide it, consult page 19. Click the triangle at right to use pop-up menu.

Toolbar. To change its size, see page 246. To hide it, see page 19.

Chain link icon. To use, see page 18.

The Netscape icon shoots stars when it's loading a page. Also, click on it to go to Netscape's home page.

Directory buttons. To hide, see page 19.

Contents. To change font, see page 20. To change the colors or background image, see page 248.

Use the scroll bars to view more of the contents area.

Drag the edges of the window to resize the browser.

Secure pages are indicated by a solid key on a blue background Click the key for more info

The status bar shows how much of a page has been loaded and sometimes contains dynamic java-defined messages about the page.

Click the letter icon to get mail *(see page 111)*.

Figure 1.3 *Choose General Preferences in the Options menu.*

Figure 1.4 *Click Home Page Location under Startup and then type the URL of the desired page.*

Choosing a home page

The first time you open a browser, Netscape jumps to the Web page that you have specified in the General Preferences dialog box. Although Netscape calls this your *home page,* don't confuse it with a Web site's home page. Instead, it is simply any page on the World Wide Web that you wish to jump to automatically upon opening Netscape. You may also set Netscape to open any HTML file on your hard disk.

To choose a home page:

1. Choose General Preferences in the Options menu **(Figure 1.3)**. The General Preferences box appears.

2. Click the Appearance tab. The Appearance preferences appear **(Figure 1.4)**.

3. In the Startup section, next to Start With, click Home Page Location and type the URL of the home page in the field directly below.

✔ Tips

■ Choose Blank Page next to Start With to have Netscape open with a blank page.

■ The home page's URL will appear in the Location field of a blank page opened upon launching Netscape. Press Enter to jump to it.

■ You can save your bookmarks file or address book as an HTML file and use that file as your home page. If your home page is on your hard disk, type **file:///c|/path/filename** in the Home Page Location field. (And yes, there are *three* forward slashes after **file:** as well as a vertical bar after *c,* which denotes your hard disk.)

Using the chain link icon

To the left of the Location field is a small chain link icon that represents the URL of the current page that you're browsing. You can use the icon to save or copy the URL into other documents.

To use the chain link icon:

■ Double click the chain link to copy the current page's URL to the clipboard.

■ Drag the chain link to the Bookmarks window—which has to be open and visible—to save a page's URL for easy future access. For more information on using the Bookmarks window, consult Chapter 8, *Bookmarks*.

■ Drag the chain link to an open word processor document **(Figure 1.5)** to copy the current page's URL to that document **(Figure 1.6)**.

■ Drag the chain link to a Web page that you are creating in the Editor window to add a link to the current page. For more information on creating links, consult Chapter 17, *Creating Links in a Page*.

■ In Windows 95, drag the chain link icon to the Desktop to create a shortcut to the current page.

✔ Tips

■ If you can't see the chain link icon, you probably don't have the Location field visible. Choose Show Location in the Options menu to make it appear.

■ You can't drag the chain link icon everywhere. You'll know it's working if the arrow shows a link icon when it's on top of the destination.

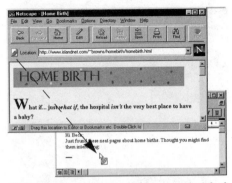

Figure 1.5 *Drag the chain link icon at the left of the Location field to the document where you want to copy the page's URL.*

Figure 1.6 *The page's URL is pasted into the selected document. (This document is from Word for Windows 6.)*

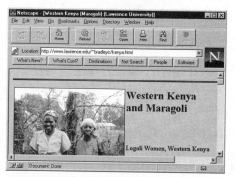

Figure 1.7 *The toolbar, location field, and directory buttons are showing, by default.*

Figure 1.8 *Choose the appropriate command from the Options menu to hide (or reveal) the corresponding feature.*

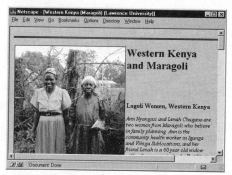

Figure 1.9 *This window is the exact same size as the one shown in Figure 1.7. Once you hide the extra window items, you see more of the actual page.*

Controlling a browser's appearance

Each browser can contain a toolbar full of buttons, a Location field, Directory buttons, and a status area **(Figure 1.7)**. You can choose to hide everything but the status area to save room on your screen and see more of your Web pages. You can also resize the window as necessary.

The toolbar contains a series of navigation and utility buttons. The Location field shows the URL address of the current Web page and can also be used to jump to different Web pages. The Directory buttons take you to particular pages on Netscape's Web site, or to other sites that Netscape has chosen for you.

To hide (or reveal) the toolbar, Location field, or Directory buttons:

Choose Show Toolbar, Show Location, or Show Directory Buttons in the Options menu to remove (or restore) the checkmark that is next to the command **(Fig. 1.8)**. The corresponding feature will disappear (or appear).The next time you open Netscape, the browser will retain the size and features you have chosen.

To resize the browser:

Drag any edge of the window to the desired size. Netscape copies the size of the last active window (even after you quit) and creates new windows based on that same size.

✔ Tip

■ To resize the buttons on the toolbar, use the General Preferences dialog box *(see page 246)*.

Choosing fonts for the browser

In an attempt to keep Web pages as universal as possible, text only appears in one of two fonts, a proportional font like Times in which individual letters have different sizes, or a fixed width font like Courier in which all the characters are the same size.

You can choose which font (and size) you wish to use for displaying proportional text and which font (and size) should be used for displaying fixed width text.

To choose fonts for the browser:

1. Choose General Preferences in the Options menu **(Fig. 1.10)**. The General Preferences dialog box appears.

2. Click the Fonts tab. The Fonts preferences are displayed **(Figure 1.11)**.

3. Click the Choose Font button next to the font you wish to specify.

4. In the Choose Base Font dialog box that appears choose the font that you wish to use **(Figure 1.12)**.

5. Choose a base size for the font.

6. Click OK to return to the Fonts preferences dialog box **(Figure 1.13)**.

7. If desired, repeat steps 3–6 to choose a font for the other style.

8. Click OK to close the dialog box.

✔ Tip

■ Most text viewed on a Web page is displayed in the proportional font. Block quotes, computer commands, and form fields are all displayed in the secondary, fixed width font.

Figure 1.10 *Choose General Preferences in the Options menu.*

Figure 1.11 *In the Fonts tab of the General Preferences dialog box, click Choose Font next to the type of font you wish to choose.*

Figure 1.12 *Select the font and size that you wish to use. Then click OK.*

Figure 1.13 *Once you've chosen a new font, it is displayed in the Fonts tab.*

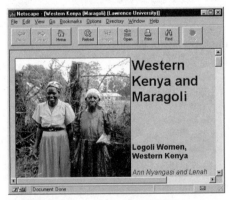

Figure 1.14 *Here's a new look at the page shown in Figure 1.7, but with Arial 12 as a base font.*

Surfing the Web

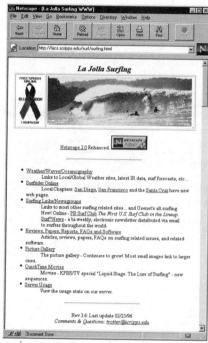

Figure 2.1 *There are over four million Web pages that you can surf to, each one different from the next.*

This is what you've been waiting for: actually getting to surf the World Wide Web. Although *surf* seems like a strange way to describe your activities as you sit in front of a computer, probably some distance from the beach, it does capture the idea of jumping from one Web page to another, perhaps reading and exploring as you go along, perhaps just enjoying the spray of information.

From its navigation buttons and keyboard shortcuts for getting from one place to another, to its clever new frames and history menu for remembering where you've been, Netscape makes surfing the Web as easy as it's ever been.

There are over four million Web sites (at press time), and several thousand more are added daily. You could spend your whole life wandering from page to page and never get to the end (although you might circle around to where you started). It's something like reading an encyclopedia from *Aardvark* to *Zen*: you'd learn a lot, but it would take you a long time.

In this section, we'll talk about how to get around on the Web with Netscape, assuming you already know where you want to go, or, on the other hand, that you don't really care where you end up. For more information on finding specific topics or pages, see Chapter 7, *Finding Stuff on the Web*.

What is a Web page?

So what are these things that you surf to? A Web page is nothing more than a text file with special tags that format the contents, point to other pages, and insert images and sounds **(Fig. 2.2)**. The tags are called *HyperText Markup Language*, or HTML, and are quite easy to learn **(Figure 2.3)**. For details on creating your own Web pages, consult *Part II: Netscape Navigator Gold* starting on page 161.

With four million Web pages in existence, there is an incredible variety of designs and approaches, and of the kinds of information presented. It is probably safe to say that you can find a Web page about any topic you might choose to research—from Contra dancing to the Ethernet, from a subway map of major cities of the world to a database of every language spoken on each train.

Some Web pages are personal, designed by a single individual with information about themselves, their family and friends, perhaps their dog or cat, and their hobbies—as well as links to their favorite pages at other sites. Personal does not mean sloppy. As you'll find out, many of the best pages are created by people with no economic interest in the Web.

Other pages are strictly—or more subtly—commercial, created by (or for) a company in order to offer promotional information, technical support, upgrades, special tips, and other benefits to the public. Often, a commercial page's mission is simply to impress—with dazzling graphics, sounds, or videos.

Each Web page has a unique address, or *URL,* which indicates its location on the Internet. For more information about URLs, consult *Links and URLs* on page 203.

Figure 2.2 *This is a typical Web page. It was written by Calvin Hamilton, a private citizen like you or me, with the sole intention of sharing information and resources across the Internet.*

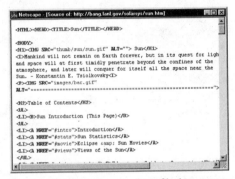

Figure 2.3 *This is the actual text file that creates the page shown in Figure 2.2. The HTML codes are those that are found within the less than and greater than signs "<>".*

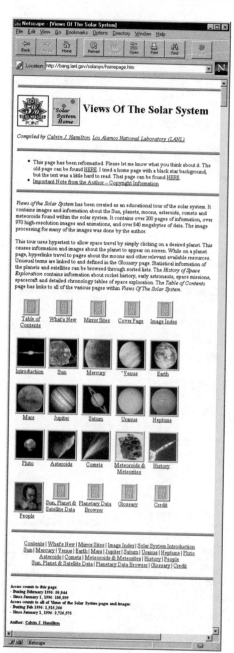

Figure 2.4 *This is the home page for the Solar System site. It contains an introduction, links to the other pages at the site, and links to related sites.*

Sites, home pages, and servers

A Web *page* is a single text file written in HTML. A Web *site* is a collection of Web pages that belong to a single individual or company. Most Web sites have a special page, called a *home page,* that serves as a door to the rest of the site **(Figure 2.4)**. A home page generally has a banner explaining what the site contains—commercial sites usually include their company logo on the home page—as well as links to the other pages available at the site.

Beware: Although Netscape Communications knows exactly what a home page is, they've chosen to use the same term to denote the page that you jump to automatically upon launching the program *(see page 17)*. The page you choose may or may not be a *real* home page.

Web pages, including any graphics, sounds, videos or other external files, are stored on *servers,* dedicated computers that are connected to the Internet 24 hours a day—so that anyone, in any part of the world, can reach the Web page at any time.

Although you might think a server looks like something out of a movie—a huge hulking thing with those reel-to-reel tapes—any kind of computer can be a server, including Macs, PCs running Windows, and most often, Unix machines. The most important criterion for a server is not size or speed, but rather that it have a high-speed connection to the Internet so that it can efficiently handle the incoming requests for the Web sites it contains.

In addition to Web sites, servers can also contain FTP and Gopher sites, and manage e-mail and Usenet newsgroups.

Following links

A Web page's most distinguishing characteristic, and certainly the feature that has made Web surfing so popular and exciting, is its *links*. By clicking a link, you jump to another page, either at the same site or at a different site—which can be on the same server or, just as easily, at a site halfway around the world. You may also use links to jump to FTP and Gopher sites and to write e-mail.

Generally, new links—that is, the ones you have not yet visited—appear underlined and in blue (or in gray on monochrome monitors). Once you have followed a link to its destination, it will appear in purple so you can quickly distinguish new links from those you've already visited.

To follow a link:

1. In the current Web page, decide which link you wish to follow. Point to the link with the mouse. The link's URL appears in the status area at the bottom of the window **(Figure 2.5)**.

2. Click the link. Netscape takes you to the link's destination **(Figure 2.6)**.

✔ Tips

■ Open the link in a new window by right clicking the link and choosing Open Link in New Window from the pop-up menu that appears.

■ You can always tell if a link is really a link by pointing at it with the mouse. If it is a link, the pointer will change into a pointing finger, and the link's destination will appear in the status area at the bottom of the browser.

Figure 2.5 *When you place the pointer over a link, which is usually blue and underlined—* Mercury *in this example, the URL for the destination page appears in the status area at the bottom left corner of the browser.*

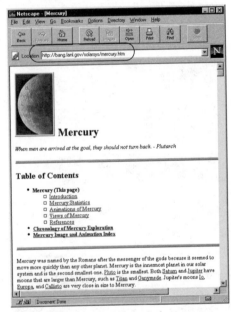

Figure 2.6 *When you click a link, Netscape loads the corresponding page. Notice how the URL in the Location field above matches the URL in the status area at the bottom left corner of Figure 2.5.*

Following links

Figure 2.7 *Choose General Preferences in the Options menu.*

Figure 2.8 *Click the Colors tab, click Custom next to Links or Followed links, and then click Choose Color.*

Figure 2.9 *Choose the desired color and click OK.*

Figure 2.10 *Click the Appearance tab and then click Underlined next to Links are in the bottom section.*

Changing the appearance of links

Most pages show new links in blue and visited links in purple. However, a Web page designer can present her links in any colors she chooses—which can sometimes be confusing. Netscape also gives *you* the ability to view links in the colors that you prefer, and to show them underlined, or not.

To change the appearance of links:

1. Choose General Preferences in the Options menu **(Figure 2.7)**. The General Preferences box appears.

2. Click the Colors tab to show the preferences for Colors **(Figure 2.8)**.

3. Click the Custom box next to the type of links that you wish to change.

4. Click the corresponding Choose Color button. The Color dialog box appears.

5. Click on a new color in the Color dialog box and then click OK to save the changes **(Fig. 2.9)**. The new color appears to the right of Custom.

6. Repeat steps 3–5 for each kind of link.

7. To ensure that the links are always displayed with the colors you have chosen, click Always Use My Colors, Overriding Document.

8. Click the Appearance tab at the top of the General Preferences dialog box.

9. In the Link Styles section, check the Underlined box to display links with an underline; uncheck the box to remove underlining **(Figure 2.10)**.

10. Click OK to save the changes.

Changing the appearance of links

Jumping to a known page

If you already know the URL of the Web that you want to visit, the best way to get to the page is to be direct: tell Netscape.

To jump to a known page:

1. Make sure the Location field is showing on the screen *(see page 19)*.

2. Type the URL of the page you want to visit in the Location field. As you begin to type, the label changes from Location to Go to **(Figure 2.11)**.

3. Press Enter. The new page appears.

✔ Tips

■ If a URL begins with *www (ftp, gopher)*, you don't need to type the protocol (**http://**, **ftp://**, or **gopher://**). Further, if a Web page address is in the form of *www.site.com*, you only need to type **site**.

■ If you don't know the URL, type a few keywords, separated by spaces. Netscape will load a search utility and will attempt to find related pages.

■ Choose New Web Browser in the File menu before going to a new page to open the page in a new browser.

■ You may jump to FTP and Gopher sites using these same techniques.

■ The last ten locations that you type into the Location field are stored in a pop-up menu to the field's right. You may jump to any of these stored locations by using the pop-up menu.

■ You can also choose the Open command in the File menu **(Fig. 2.13)** and type the URL in the Open Location dialog box that appears **(Figure 2.14)**.

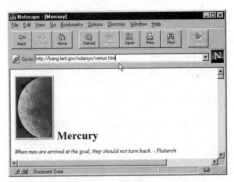

Figure 2.11 *In the Location field between the toolbar and the content area, type the URL of the desired page. As soon as you begin to type, the word* Location *changes to* Go to.

Figure 2.12 *Netscape loads the specified page.*

Figure 2.13 *Choose Open Location in the File menu.*

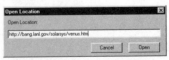

Figure 2.14 *In the Open Location dialog box that appears, type the URL of the page that you wish to jump to.*

Figure 2.15 *Supposing you are at point E, the Go menu will contain points F, E, C, B, and A, in that order. D (and all the other branches) will be forgotten. Going forward will bring you to F. Going backward will bring you to C. Going backward again will bring you to B.*

☆You are here

Going back and forward

Perhaps one of the most difficult problems you'll have on the Web is following all of the links that interest you. Typically, you will find one Web page with several links that you want to follow. It's important to know how to get *back* to the page with the important links, once you've explored one or more of them **(Figure 2.15)**.

To go back to the previous page:

Click the Back button on the toolbar **(Figure 2.16)** or choose Back in the Go menu **(Figure 2.17)**. Netscape will load the page that you visited immediately before jumping to the present page **(Figure 2.18)**.

Figure 2.16 *Click the Back button to return to the last page you were browsing.*

Figure 2.17 *You can choose Back from the Go menu to get the same result.*

Going back means returning to the pages that brought you to the present page. *Going forward*, then, is turning around once again and following the same path that you did before. It's something like going back to where you came back from.

There are two conditions to going forward. First, you have to have gone back before you can go forward. Second, you must not have chosen a new link on an earlier page that brings you in a new direction. Since Netscape only remembers one path at a time, if you switch paths, all the most forward pages are forgotten.

To go forward:

Click the Forward button or choose Forward in the Go menu. Netscape will bring you to the corresponding page.

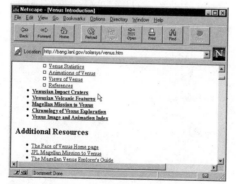

Figure 2.18 *In this example, Netscape goes back to the Venus Introduction page, which, as you can see in Figure 2.17 is before the current page (Venusian Impact Craters) in the Go menu.*

Going further back or further ahead

As you wander around the Web, Netscape records the title and URL of each page that you visit and stores it in the Go menu. You can go back and revisit a page by choosing its title in the menu.

To go further back or further ahead:

Select the desired page from the Go menu **(Figure 2.19)**. Netscape jumps to the corresponding page **(Figure 2.20)**.

✔ Tips

■ Unfortunately, the Go menu only keeps track of the path of pages that has brought you to the current page. So if you backtrack (with the Back command or the Go menu) and then choose a link that leads you in a different direction, the references to the *later* pages will be lost **(Fig. 2.21)**.

■ One way to make sure the Go menu keeps track of *every* page you visit is to avoid using the Back and Forward commands and even the Go menu itself. If you need to go back to a page you have already visited, use the Open Location command instead.

■ To record a page's URL permanently, create a bookmark for it. For more details, see Chapter 8, *Bookmarks*.

■ Although the History window contains the same information as the Go menu, you may prefer to use it since it floats quietly on your screen—always at your fingertips. For more information, consult *Using the History window* on page 29.

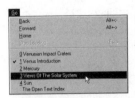

Figure 2.19 *You can choose any page in the Go menu to jump to that page.*

Figure 2.20 *A page that is loaded from the Go menu often appears faster than a brand new page since Netscape has already saved a copy of the page in its memory cache. In addition, when using the Go menu or Back and Forward commands you always return to the area of the page that you last visited.*

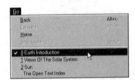

Figure 2.21 *If you backtrack and then set off in a new direction (as in this case, going back from Venus to the home page and from there, on to Earth) and then view the Go menu, the old path (that led to the Venus page) will no longer be shown.*

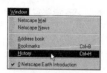

Figure 2.22 *Choose History in the Window menu to show the History window.*

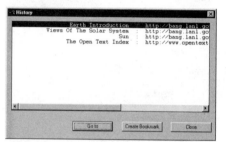

Figure 2.23 *The History window lets you see the pages that you have visited in the current session. You can jump to any page in the current session by double clicking it and add a bookmark by choosing the Create Bookmark button.*

Figure 2.24 *When you type* **about:global** *in the Location field, Netscape displays the URLs of all the files that you have recently displayed in the browser.*

Using the History window

Netscape's History window keeps track of your travels on the Web. Each time you jump to a new page, the page's URL and title are added to the History window. However, the History window, like the Go menu, only keeps track of one path of pages at a time. That is, if you backtrack and then follow a new link in a new direction, all the pages after that page will be erased from the History window.

To use the History window:

1. Choose History in the Window menu **(Figure 2.22)** to view the History window **(Figure 2.23)**.

2. Double click on a page to jump to that page. You can also click once and then click the Go to button.

3. Click on a page and then click Create Bookmark to add a bookmark for that page to your Bookmarks window. For more information on bookmarks, see Chapter 8, *Bookmarks*.

4. To close the History window, simply click the Close button.

✔ Tips

■ If you have the History window open as you backtrack, an arrow appears next to the current page in the History window, while the pages further ahead on the path remain visible.

■ If you want to see everywhere you've been, type **about:global** in the Location field and press Enter. Netscape will show the URLs for all the places you've recently visited **(Figure 2.24)**. The Followed Links option determines how many are remembered *(see page 246).*

Using the History window

Going to *your* home page

You can return to the home page that you specified in the General Preferences dialog box at any time with a simple click. For information on how to set your home page, consult *Choosing a home page* on page 17.

To go to your home page:

Click the Home button in the tool bar **(Figure 2.25)** or choose Home in the Go menu **(Figure 2.26)**. Netscape loads the home page specified in the Appearance tab of the General Preferences dialog box **(Figure 2.27)**.

✔ Tips

■ Remember, the Home button and Home menu commands bring you to *your* specified home page, not to the home page of the site that contains the page you are currently viewing (which would be much more useful, if you ask me).

■ Further, even if you have specified that Netscape *start* with a blank page, the program will still jump to the page specified in the General Preferences box when you use the Home button or command.

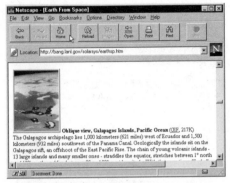

Figure 2.25 *Click the Home button to load the page specified in the General Preferences dialog box (not the site's home page).*

Figure 2.26 *You can also choose Home in the Go menu to load your home page.*

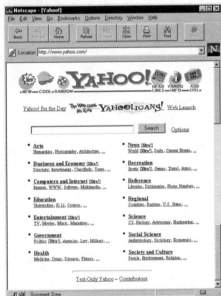

Figure 2.27 *A home page should either be a page that you consult often, or a page with a lot of links to other pages.*

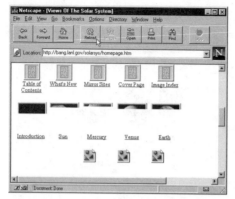

Figure 2.28 *Click the Reload button to have Netscape consult the server for any changes and to update the page accordingly. The Reload button also comes in handy if you've stopped the page from loading in mid-transfer, as shown.*

Figure 2.29 *You can also choose Reload in the View menu to have Netscape update the page.*

Figure 2.30 *Once the page is reloaded, the images and text appear in full.*

Figure 2.31 *Choose Refresh to get rid of any screen redraw related deformations.*

Reloading and refreshing a page

When you jump to a page, Netscape automatically loads a copy of the page into its memory cache. The *next* time you jump to the page, instead of asking the server for the information (which might be rather slow, depending on the type of connection you have and the type of server that contains the page), it loads the page from memory.

However, if you suspect (or know) that the contents of the page have changed, if the page has not loaded completely, or if it has not loaded properly, you will want Netscape to load the page from the server and not from memory.

To reload a page:

Click the Reload button **(Figure 2.28)** or choose Reload in the View menu **(Figure 2.29)**. Netscape updates the page's contents **(Figure 2.30)**.

Sometimes, Netscape fails to view a page correctly, perhaps not aligning or displaying the text properly. In this case, even if you don't think the page's contents have changed, you may wish to refresh the page to view it properly.

To refresh a page:

Choose Refresh in the View menu **(Figure 2.31)**. Netscape refreshes the page and redraws the screen.

✔ Tip

■ You can force a reload, regardless of the status of a page, by holding down the Alt key and selecting Super Reload in the View menu.

Stopping a page from loading

As you get used to working with Netscape you'll get a feel for how fast it moves from one page to another and how long it takes average pages to load. There are three principal reasons why you might want to abort a jump to a page. First, you may simply have changed your mind, or made an errant click. Second, the page may be taking so long that you decide to go somewhere else. Finally, you may notice, as you watch the status bar, that Netscape takes an unusually long time to connect to the host. This is a good clue that either the server is busy or that the page is no longer located where you thought it was. Just abort the jump and move on.

To stop a page from loading:

1. Click the Stop button on the toolbar **(Figure 2.32)** or choose Stop Loading in the Go menu **(Figure 2.33)**. Netscape immediately stops trying to load the page and shows you what it's come up with so far, if anything. The word "Done" should appear in the status bar at the bottom left area of the window and the Netscape icon should stop shooting comets.

2. If part of the page has already loaded, and if you decide you really do want to continue loading the page, click the Reload button, or choose Reload in the View menu, to load the entire page *(see page 31)*.

✔ Tip

■ You can also press Esc to stop loading a page.

Figure 2.32 *You can stop a page from loading completely by clicking the Stop button.*

Figure 2.33 *You can also choose Stop Loading in the Go menu to break the communication between Netscape and the page's server.*

Figure 2.34 *When you stop a page from loading completely, the images may appear as icons.*

Figure 2.35 *Choose Auto Load Images in the Options menu. A checkmark means the option is active. When the checkmark is absent, the images will not be loaded automatically.*

Viewing images on the Web

The two most common kinds of images that you'll find on the Web are GIF and JPEG images. Netscape can open both of these kinds of images automatically. However, since images tend to be large (and are always larger than text), they can take a long time to download and view. By default, Netscape automatically downloads all the JPEG and GIF images on the pages that you jump to. If you have a particularly slow connection, you may want to view only the text.

Figure 2.36 *With the Auto Load Images option off, the images are replaced with icons.*

To deactivate automatic image download:

Choose Auto Load Images in the Options menu to remove the checkmark from the command **(Figure 2.35)**. The next time you jump to a page, the images will be displayed with placeholders **(Fig. 2.36)**.

When you have the Auto Load Images command deactivated, you can choose to load all the images in a particular page, or to load one or more individual images.

Figure 2.37 *Load an individual image by right clicking it and choosing Load this Image.*

To load a particular image:

Right click the desired image and choose Load this Image in the pop-up menu **(Figure 2.37)**. Netscape displays the corresponding image **(Figure 2.38)**.

To load all the images on a page:

Choose Load Images in the View menu. All of the placeholders are replaced by the corresponding images. You can also click the Load Images button on the toolbar.

Figure 2.38 *The selected image is loaded.*

Viewing information about a document

You may want to get more information about a page, including the images it contains, its MIME type, when it was last modified, how big it is, what character set was used to create it and what its security level is. You can find out all this information with the Document Info command.

To view information about a document:

1. Navigate to the desired page **(Figure 2.39)**.

2. Choose Document Info in the View menu **(Figure 2.40)**. Netscape displays a window with information about the document **(Figure 2.41)**.

✔ Tips

■ Although the Document Info window has no menus, you can copy information from it using the keyboard shortcut (Ctrl+C).

■ You can jump to the images and links shown in the Document Info window by clicking them the regular way *(see page 24).*

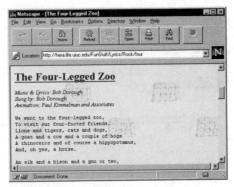

Figure 2.39 *Navigate to the desired page.*

Figure 2.40 *Choose Document Info in the View menu.*

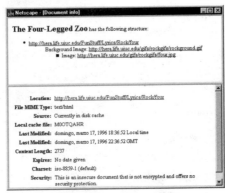

Figure 2.41 *Netscape displays information about the current page.*

Frames

Figure 3.1 *A frame is a regular page with its own URL (like the one above) that is fit into a frameset like the one in Figure 3.2.*

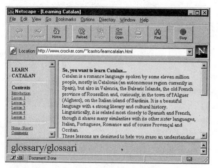

Figure 3.2 *A frameset is a page that is divided into individual frames, each of which displays the information from its own URL.*

Figure 3.3 *Oftentimes when you click a link in one frame, the corresponding URL is shown in one of the other frames, while all the remaining frames remain constant.*

With version 2, Netscape introduced frames, an ingenious feature that divides each window into individual panes that each hold their own URL. Frames make it easy to hold on to one page (say, that contains a series of links, like a table of contents) while viewing a whole series of others (where the links lead). Navigating such sites can be confusing; this chapter should make it easier to get around.

Frames and framesets

A *frame* is nothing more than a regular Web page that has been shoe-horned into a smaller area within another Web page, called a *frameset*. The frameset contains information about the size of the frames within it, including their sizes, names, scrolling qualities, and URLs **(Figure 3.2)**.

When you click on a link inside a frame, one of two things can happen. If the link is to a page at the same site, it will usually appear inside the currently open frameset, replacing the contents of one of the existing frames. The other frames remain unchanged so that you can still see the information that they contain **(Fig. 3.3)**.

If the link is to a page at a different site, the page will usually open up in a new window. If it doesn't and you want it to, consult *Opening a frame in a new window* on page 37.

Perhaps the most important thing to remember is that you, the Web surfer, cannot create or add frames to an existing page. You can only navigate the frames that are already there.

Following a link in a frame

Following a link on a page with frames is practically identical to following links on regular pages *(see page 24)*: simply click and go. The difference is in where the result will be displayed. When you click on a link in a frameset, the link is usually opened in one of the frames, while the other frames remain unchanged.

To follow a link in a frame:

1. Place the pointer over the link that you wish to jump to **(Figure 3.4)**. You may have to scroll around in the frame to make the link visible.

2. Click the link. Netscape brings you to the link's destination **(Figure 3.5)**. Many times, the page will be displayed inside one of the frames in the current frameset.

✔ Tips

■ You can't open a link in a specific frame unless the designer has allowed for it, but you can open the link in a new window *(see page 37)*.

■ Usually, a frameset contains a narrow frame with links, a central frame where those links are displayed and sometimes a static frame that contains a logo or toolbar.

■ You can often resize frames to better suit your needs. For more information, consult *Resizing and scrolling around a frame* on page 38.

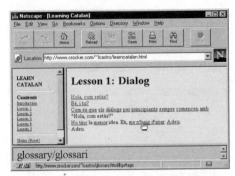

Figure 3.4 *Follow a link in one of the frames in the usual way, by positioning the cursor over the link until it turns into a hand and clicking the mouse.*

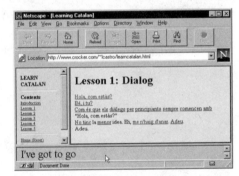

Figure 3.5 *In this example, the corresponding page is displayed in the bottom frame.*

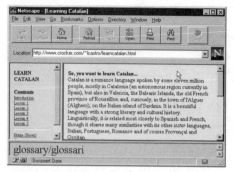

Figure 3.6 *Click in the frame (not on a link) to select it. Note the black border around the frame.*

Figure 3.7 *Choose New Web Browser in the File menu.*

Figure 3.8 *The selected frame is displayed in the new browser.*

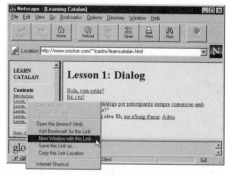

Figure 3.9 *Right click a link to the frame and choose New Window with this Link.*

Opening a frame in a new window

Often, links are *targeted* to particular frames. That means that when you click the link, the corresponding URL appears within a specific frame. If the frame is too small or too unwieldy, you may wish to open the link in a separate, independent window.

To open a frame in a new window:

1. Click in the desired frame (anywhere except over a link) to select it. A black border appears around the frame to show it is selected **(Figure 3.6)**.

2. Choose New Web Browser in the File menu **(Figure 3.7)**. Netscape opens a new browser and fills it with the selected frame **(Figure 3.8)**.

✔ Tips

■ If there is a link to the frame that you want to open in a new window, you can right click the link and then choose New Window with this Link in the pop-up menu that appears **(Figure 3.9)**.

■ Sloppy Web page designers sometimes make links to external sites appear inside a frame. If the external site happens to have its own frames, the whole frameset will be stuffed into the frame on the original page. The best thing to do is go back *(see page 39)* and then open the link in a new window.

Opening a frame in a new window

Resizing and scrolling around a frame

Depending on how the Web page designer has written the HTML for the frameset, a frame can either have a fixed size (in pixels), a relative size (that depends on the size of the whole browser), or be adjustable by the user.

In my opinion, since there is no way to foresee what size browser a user will have, designers should always make frames adjustable. Unfortunately, not all Web page designers agree.

To resize a frame:

1. Place the pointer over one of the borders of the frame **(Figure 3.10)**. If it changes into a double pointed arrow, you can change the size of the frame.

2. Drag the border to the desired new position **(Figure 3.11)**.

Similarly, a designer can create a frameset so that a frame has scroll bars all the time, none of the time, or only when necessary.

To scroll around a frame:

1. If the scroll bars are visible, click on the up or down arrows to see more information at the top or bottom of the frame, respectively. Drag the scroll box to move more quickly. Click in the gray area to move one frame area at a time **(Figure 3.12)**.

2. Or, select the frame (by clicking in it) and use the arrow keys to move around the frame.

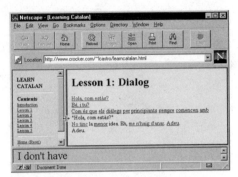

Figure 3.10 *Place the cursor between the frames. When it changes to a double-pointed arrow, drag it to resize the frames.*

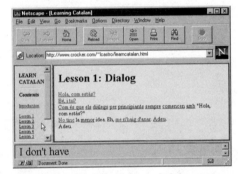

Figure 3.11 *The left column is slightly narrower now.*

Click the up arrow to move up in the frame.
Click the gray area to move down one frame's worth at a time.
Drag the scroll box to move as much as you want.
Click the bottom arrow to move down

Figure 3.12 *The scroll bars (if they're visible) let you move around the frame to see additional information.*

Figure 3.13 *After clicking on Lesson 1 and showing the corresponding frame, you may want to go back to the information previously contained in that frame.*

Figure 3.14
Choose Back or Forward in the Go menu to navigate from frame to frame. Note that the individual frames are not *listed at the bottom of the menu.*

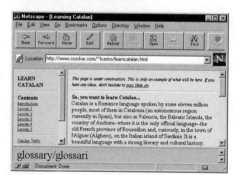

Figure 3.15 *The previous contents of the most recently changed frame are shown. The other frames remain unchanged.*

Going backward or forward in a frame

One nice change in version 3 of Netscape is that the Back and Forward buttons affect the last frame that has changed, and not just entire Web pages or framesets. Thus, if you have viewed several different pages in a particular frame, you can use the Back button to see the previous ones (and the Forward button to see later ones). In version 2, the Back and Forward buttons always affected an entire page or frameset; it was necessary to use the pop-up menu to go back in a frame.

To go backward or forward in a frame:

Choose Back or Forward in the Go menu **(Figure 3.14)**. Netscape changes the last changed frame to its previous contents **(Figure 3.15)**.

✔ Tips

- You can also use the Back and Forward buttons on the toolbar or right click the page and choose Back or Forward in the pop-up menu that appears.

- Neither the Go menu nor the History window displays the addresses for individual frames, and so you cannot jump to a specific frame directly.

Getting information about a frame

In the same way you can get information about an entire page, you can get information about an individual frame. In addition, you can get information for a frameset—and see all the frames it contains.

To get information about a frame:

1. Select the frame by clicking it **(Figure 3.16)**.

2. Choose Frame Info in the View menu **(Figure 3.17)**. Netscape displays the information for the selected frame **(Figure 3.18)**.

✔ Tips

■ If the Frame Info command in the View menu is not available, you probably haven't selected a frame.

■ To get information about the entire frameset, choose Document Info instead of Frame Info **(Figure 3.19)**.

■ Although the Frame Info window has no menu bars, you can copy material with the keyboard shortcut (Ctrl+C).

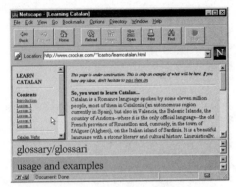

Figure 3.16 *Select the frame that you want to get information for by clicking it.*

Figure 3.17 *Choose Frame Info in the View menu.*

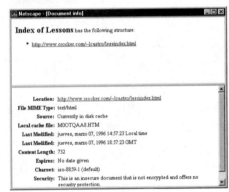

Figure 3.18 *Netscape displays the information about the frame in a new window.*

Figure 3.19 *If you choose Document Info for a frameset, you'll get information on all the frames.*

Plug-ins and Helpers

Plug-ins

Originally, Netscape could show only text and GIF images in its own browser. To expand its abilities without ballooning in size, Netscape relies on helper applications *(see page 44)* and plug-ins.

Plug-ins add features to Netscape itself, without making you go to a different program. A plug-in for audio, for example, might let you listen to a specific audio format from within Netscape's browser. The plug-in may be completely invisible, or it may add certain commands to Netscape's browser.

From version 2 on, Netscape has encouraged other companies to develop plug-ins for Netscape Navigator so that it can handle complicated images, video, sound, and other kinds of files within Netscape's own browser window.

Shipping with Netscape 3 are plug-ins for audio (LiveAudio), video (LiveVideo), teleconferencing (CoolTalk), and others. At present, there are over 130 plug-ins available, most of which were not lucky enough to be included in the main Netscape software package. You can get a complete list of available plug-ins at **http://home.netscape.com/comprod/ products/navigator/version_2.0/ plugins/index.html**.

Plug-ins

Using LiveVideo

One of Netscape 3's new plug-ins, Live-Video, is designed to let you view AVI movies that have either been embedded or linked to the Web page you've jumped to—within the page itself.

To use LiveVideo:

1. Jump to a page that has an embedded or linked AVI movie. The movie is automatically downloaded to your hard disk.

2. Click on the movie to play it **(Figure 4.1)**; click again to stop playing. (You can also right click the movie and choose Play or Pause from the pop-up menu.)

3. To rewind the movie to the beginning, right click the movie and choose Rewind **(Figure 4.2)**. To fast forward the movie to the end, right click the movie and choose Forward.

4. Advance the movie one frame forward by right clicking the movie and choosing Frame Forward in the pop-up menu. Go back one frame by choosing Frame Back in the menu.

✔ Tips

■ Despite Netscape's claims, you cannot view movies "instantly" with Live-Video. Movies are large files and take a long time to download—two or three minutes for a five second short, for example. Although you can view the rest of the page while the movie is downloading, you can't play the movie until the download is complete.

■ Movies are stored in cache. Once they're downloaded, you can go back and view them again.

Figure 4.1 *Once the movie has been downloaded, click it to view it inside the Netscape browser.*

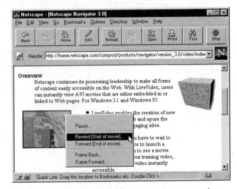

Figure 4.2 *Right click the movie to access the options in the pop-up menu.*

Figure 4.3 *Once the sound file has been downloaded, the console appears. Click the play button to start hearing the sound. (This page is from Paramount's Mission Impossible site.)*

Figure 4.4 *Right click the console and choose Save As to save the sound file to your hard disk.*

Using LiveAudio

LiveAudio, a plug-in included with the Netscape 3 package, lets you listen to audio files from within Netscape's browser.

To use LiveAudio:

1. Jump to a page with a LiveAudio link. Once the sound file is completely downloaded, a console appears **(Figure 4.3)**.

2. Click the play button to listen to the sound. Click the pause button to stop the sound without rewinding. Click the stop button to completely stop playing the sound.

3. To save a sound, right click the sound and choose Save As in the pop-up menu **(Figure 4.4)**.

✔ Tips

■ You can also right click a sound and choose Play, Pause, or Stop in the pop-up menu.

■ Sounds are large files and may take a considerable amount of time to download. LiveAudio, despite Netscape's claims, does not give "instant" access to sound. It simply gives you access from within Netscape's browser window. Personally, I'm much more fond of the helper application, RealAudio, which approximates a real radio station by downloading and playing sound files almost simultaneously (www.realaudio.com).

Helper applications

Helper applications are small, dedicated applications used for opening and viewing multimedia files outside of Netscape's browser. Helper apps (as they're affectionately known) can often be downloaded for free via FTP. There are helper apps for decompressing files, viewing PostScript files, viewing video and images, listening to sounds, and more.

Theoretically, you can use any application that you have (even Word or Photoshop, for example) as a helper app. However, since your main aim is to *view* information, you'll want something that opens quickly and immediately shows you what you need.

Common helper apps for Windows:

Type	Name
Graphics	LView Pro
	Paintshop Pro
Sound	Wham, Wplany
	RealAudio
Video	Media Player
	mpegplay
PostScript	ghostscript
	ghostview
PDF	Amber

You can find helper apps to download on many pages all over the Web. For more help, consult Chapter 7, *Finding Stuff on the Web.*

Figure 4.5 *If you click a link to a multimedia file that Netscape can't open on its own or with a plug-in, it will launch a helper application to deal with the file.*

Figure 4.6 *Netscape automatically downloads the files that it can't read on its own.*

Figure 4.7 *Once the file has finished downloading, Netscape launches the helper application which opens the file and displays it. This is a movie of the Earth rotating.*

Figure 4.8 *Choose General Preferences in the Options menu.*

Figure 4.9 *Choose the desired file type in the list, click Launch Application and then click Browse.*

Figure 4.10 *Find the helper application on your hard disk and click OK.*

Figure 4.11 *The helper application's name and icon are shown at the bottom of the General Preferences dialog box.*

Setting up helper apps

Once you've downloaded the helper applications on your hard disk, you must tell Netscape where they can be found and which ones should be used with which files.

To set up helper apps:

1. Choose General Preferences in the Options menu **(Figure 4.8)**. The General Preferences box appears.

2. Click the Helpers tab to view the Helpers apps preferences.

3. Select the file type that you wish to associate with a particular helper application **(Figure 4.9)**.

4. Next to Action, choose Launch the Application.

5. Click Browse. A dialog box appears in which you can indicate the name and location of the helper application.

6. Locate the helper app and click Open **(Figure 4.10)**. The program's icon, if it has one, appears next to its path and file name in the Helpers tab **(Figure 4.11)**.

7. Repeat steps 3–6 for each helper app you wish to assign to a particular kind of file.

✔ Tip

■ Some installers complete this process for you. Check the helper app's documentation to be sure.

Setting up helper apps

When no helper app is available

There may be many kinds of files that you never—or rarely—encounter and for which you don't have the corresponding helper application. In this case, you can have Netscape either save the file to disk or ask you what program to use to open the file.

To set options when no helper app is available:

1. Choose General Preferences in the Options menu **(Figure 4.12)**.

2. Click the Helpers tab to view the Helpers apps preferences.

3. Select the file type that you want to set options for **(Figure 4.13)**.

4. Next to Action, choose Save to Disk if you want Netscape to automatically save the file to your hard disk. Choose Unknown: Prompt User to have Netscape alert you each time it encounters a file it doesn't know what to do with.

5. Click OK to save the changes.

✔ Tips

■ You might want to use the Save to Disk option for files from another platform that you don't want to open on the present computer.

■ Netscape automatically views text files in the browser. To automatically save text files, select the *text/plain* file type and then choose Save to Disk. Don't choose Save to Disk for *text/ html* files, or you won't be able to view Web pages.

Figure 4.12 *Choose General Preferences in the Options menu.*

Figure 4.13 *Select the desired file type and then click either Save to Disk or Unknown: Prompt User in the Action section.*

Transferring Files

In order to transfer files from one computer to another, for example, from a server in New Jersey to your house, the two computers need to speak to each other the same way—with the same *protocol*. Before the Web, the most common protocols for downloading files were FTP (which stands for *file transfer protocol*) and Gopher. And even though today it's quite simple to download files from a Web page, most servers continue to offer files through the two older systems.

Netscape allows you to access FTP or Gopher servers in much the same way as you would regular Web servers by displaying their contents as a series of hierarchical folders.

FTP and Gopher servers do not have links to other sites, and generally they don't include explanatory text. They are dedicated to file transfer. Some sites are open to the public, while others are restricted to particular users.

To transfer files to another person or company via e-mail, consult *Attaching files to a message* on page 126.

Accessing an FTP site

Many servers offer either anonymous or private FTP. Universities, Internet service providers, and computer manufacturers typically offer anonymous FTP access to their files, which may be doctoral dissertations, Web software or program updates, respectively, among many other possibilities. In addition, you may have access to a private FTP site at your own server.

Figure 5.1 *Select Open Location in the File menu or click the Open button on the tool-*

To access an FTP site:

1. Choose Open Location in the File menu or click the Open button on the toolbar **(Figure 5.1)**. The Open Location dialog box appears.

2. For an anonymous FTP site, type **ftp://ftp.site** where *ftp.site* is the URL address of the desired FTP site **(Figure 5.2)**. To access a private FTP site, you'll have to type **ftp://user name:password@ftp.site**.

3. Click Open. Netscape contacts the FTP server and displays the contents of the FTP site **(Figure 5.3)**.

✔ Tips

- You can also type the FTP address in the Location text box under the toolbar, if it is showing *(see page 19)*.

- If the anonymous FTP address begins with the word *ftp*, you don't need to type the initial **ftp://**; Netscape will add it automatically **(Figure 5.4)**.

- Anonymous FTP sites often limit the number of people that can connect at a time. If you get an error message, try again later. According to Internet etiquette, you shouldn't access a university site during business hours.

Figure 5.2 *Type the FTP address in the Open Location dialog box.*

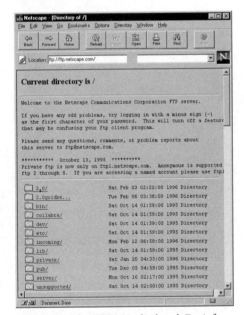

Figure 5.3 *The FTP site is displayed. For information on downloading files, see page 50.*

Figure 5.4 *You only have to begin the URL with* ftp:// *if the FTP address does not begin with the letters* ftp.

Accessing an FTP site

Figure 5.5 *Select Open Location in the File menu or click the Open button on the toolbar.*

Figure 5.6 *Type the URL of the desired Gopher site in the Open Location dialog box.*

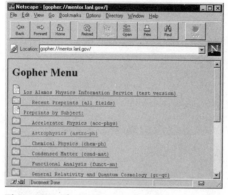

Figure 5.7 *The Gopher site is displayed. For information on downloading files, see page 50.*

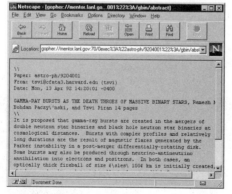

Figure 5.8 *When you click a text document, it is displayed in the browser.*

Accessing a Gopher site

The Gopher protocol, supported by many university sites, lets you search databases and retrieve files. Although there continues to be wide support for Gopher, it has been generally supplanted by the Web.

To access a Gopher site:

1. Choose Open Location in the File menu or click the Open button on the toolbar **(Figure 5.5)**. The Open Location dialog box appears.

2. Type **gopher://gopher.site** where *gopher.site* is the URL address of the desired Gopher site **(Figure 5.6)**.

3. Click Open. Netscape contacts the Gopher server and displays the available files on screen **(Figure 5.7)**.

4. Click on a folder to see its contents. Click on a text file to display it **(Figure 5.8)**.

✔ Tips

■ If the Gopher address begins with the word *gopher*, you don't need to type the initial **gopher://**; Netscape will add it automatically.

■ You can also type the Gopher address in the Location bar in the main Netscape window, if it is showing *(see page 19)*.

Accessing a Gopher site

Downloading files

Once you have accessed the desired FTP, Gopher, or Web site, actually downloading a file is only a click away.

To download a file:

1. Access the desired site.

2. Click on the appropriate folders until you find the file you wish to download **(Figure 5.9)**.

3. Click the desired file. Netscape may ask you what to do with the file. Click Save File to save it to your hard disk **(Figure 5.10)**.

4. In the Save As dialog box that appears, choose the directory in which to save the file and click Save **(Figure 5.11)**.

5. Netscape initiates the transfer and shows the Save file dialog box which indicates the size of the file and how long it will take to download **(Figure 5.12)**.

6. If you change your mind about downloading the file, click the Cancel button in the Save file dialog box.

✔ Tips

■ Netscape automatically displays text files in the browser instead of saving them. To save a text file, right click it and choose Save this Link as in the pop-up menu. For more information, consult *Saving a page without jumping to it* on page 55.

■ You can set up Netscape so that it saves and/or uncompresses certain kinds of files automatically. For more information, consult *Helper applications* on page 44.

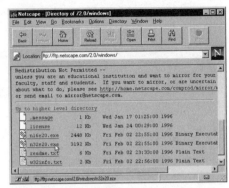

Figure 5.9 *Find the file that you wish to download from a site. You may have to wade through several layers of folders. Click the file to download it. Text files are automatically displayed in the browser.*

Figure 5.10 *Netscape may ask you want you want to do with the selected file. Click Save File to save it to your hard disk.*

Figure 5.11 *Choose the directory on your hard disk in which you wish to save the file and click Save.*

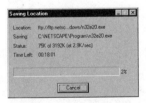

Figure 5.12 *The Saving Location dialog box tells you how large the file is, gives you an estimate of how long it will take to download (and how much has been downloaded so far), and lets you cancel the download if you change your mind.*

Figure 5.13 *Navigate to the FTP site where you want to upload the file.*

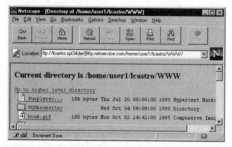

Figure 5.14 *Open the directory in which you wish to save the file (here, WWW).*

Figure 5.15 *Choose Upload File in the File menu.*

Figure 5.16 *Choose the file on your hard disk that you wish to upload. Click Open.*

Uploading a file with FTP

Although you can download a file from an FTP, Gopher, or Web site, you can usually only upload a file to an FTP site. You might want to upload a Web page that you've created to your Internet service provider's server so that other users can have access to it. Or a software manufacturer might ask you to upload a file that lists your system extensions so that they can help you with a bombing program.

To upload a file with FTP:

1. Access the FTP site and navigate to the desired folder in which you wish to upload the file **(Figure 5.13 and Figure 5.14)**.

2. Choose Upload file in the File menu **(Figure 5.15)**.

3. In the dialog box that appears—that displays the contents of your hard disk—choose the desired file and click Open **(Figure 5.16)**. The file is transferred to the FTP site.

4. If you change your mind about uploading the file, click the Cancel button in the File Upload dialog box or the Stop button on the toolbar.

✔ Tips

■ You may continue using Netscape while you are uploading a file. Of course, it won't be as fast as if it were dedicated to the one task.

■ Be careful when you upload files. Once you've uploaded them, you can't change their location with Netscape. Of course, you can use a dedicated FTP client like Win_ftp to move files around on the FTP server.

Uploading a file with FTP

Uploading multiple files

If you use Netscape 2 with Windows 95, you can upload several files at once to an FTP site using drag and drop. You can drag files from the desktop, or from the Explorer, whichever is easier.

To upload multiple files:

1. Connect to your FTP site *(see page 48)* and navigate to the desired destination directory.

2. Select the desired files on the desktop or in the Explorer.

3. Drag the files to the Netscape browser showing the FTP site. When the pointer gains a plus sign, release the mouse button **(Figure 5.17)**.

4. Click the Netscape browser to make it active. An alert appears asking if you wish to upload the dragged files to the FTP site **(Figure 5.18)**.

5. Click OK in the alert. The files are uploaded.

✔ Tip

■ Although you *can* use the File Manager to drag files to the FTP site, you probably shouldn't. It will truncate file names to the 8.3 format—using .htm instead of .html— and convert them to all upper case. I've also had some problems dragging items from the Explorer that were created in a non-Windows 95 compliant program. Although the Explorer *shows* these files with upper and lower case letters, it drags them all upper case. The safest bet is to drag the files from a folder on the Desktop.

Figure 5.17 *Drag the desired files from a folder on the desktop to the open Netscape browser, showing the FTP site.*

Figure 5.18 *Click on the Netscape browser and this alert appears. Click OK to complete the transfer.*

Saving and Printing

As you surf, you may find images and text that you would like to save. Although much of the material on the Web is copyrighted, you are allowed to save files for your own use—for example, to read a page or view an image after you have disconnected from your online service.

The images that you find on Web pages can only be saved in their original format. You will have to use a separate program like Paintshop Pro or Adobe Photoshop to convert them to other formats.

If you find a particularly interesting page and you want to keep a copy of it, or share it with someone who's (gasp) not on the Web, you can print out a copy.

Saving a Web page

Netscape can save a Web page with or without its HTML tags. To open the file with a word processor and work with the data in some way, you should save the page *without* HTML tags—Netscape calls this "Plain Text" format.

To read the page with Netscape once you've disconnected from your online service, or to study other peoples' HTML, you should save the file *with* HTML tags—Netscape calls this "HTML Files" format.

To save a Web page:

1. Jump to the desired page **(Fig. 6.1)**.

2. Choose Save As in the File menu **(Fig. 6.2)**. The Save As box appears.

3. In the Save File as Type submenu at the bottom of the dialog box **(Fig. 6.3)**, choose HTML Files to save the page with HTML tags, or Plain Text to save the page without HTML tags.

4. Give the file a name and click OK. A progress bar indicates how long it will take **(Figure 6.4)**.

✔ Tips

■ If you save the file in HTML Files format, Netscape automatically adds the extension .htm to the file name so that all browsers on all platforms can recognize the file.

■ Don't be confused by Netscape's use of *Plain Text*. All Web pages—even those saved with HTML tags in HTML Files format—are text files.

■ Images are not downloaded when you save a page unless you have Netscape Gold *(see page 168)*. To save images with "plain" Netscape, see page 56.

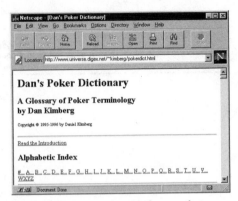

Figure 6.1 *First, navigate to the page that you want to save.*

Figure 6.2 *Choose Save As in the File menu.*

Figure 6.3 *Choose either HTML Files or Plain Text in the Save File as Type pop-up menu, give the file a name (or use the existing one) and then click OK.*

Figure 6.4 *The Saving Location dialog box indicates how long it will take to save the file to disk.*

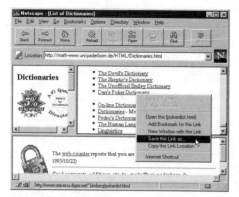

Figure 6.5 *First, navigate to the page that contains a link to the page you want to save. Right click the link and then choose Save this Link as in the pop-up menu.*

Figure 6.6 *Choose either HTML Files or Plain Text in the Save File as Type pop-up menu, give the file a name (or use the existing one) and then click OK.*

Saving a page without jumping to it

You can save a Web page without even navigating to it. This is convenient when you are on a page with several links to other interesting looking pages, since you can save each of the other pages without leaving the main page that has the links.

To save a page without jumping to it:

1. Jump to a page that contains a link to the page you wish to save.

2. Right click the link and choose Save this Link as in the pop-up menu **(Figure 6.5)**.

3. In the Save File as Type submenu at the bottom of the Save As box that appears, choose HTML Files to save the page with HTML tags, or Plain Text to save the page without HTML tags **(Figure 6.6)**.

4. Change the file name if desired and click OK.

✔ Tips

■ If you save the file in HTML Files format, Netscape automatically adds the extension .htm to the file name so that all browsers on all platforms can recognize the file.

■ Hold down the Shift key and right click a link to save the corresponding page without using the pop-up menu.

■ Use the original file names if you want the internal links between a set of related pages to work offline.

Saving an image

Inline images are not downloaded automatically when you save a Web page. You must save each image separately.

External images, on the other hand, are usually downloaded to your hard disk automatically when you view them. For more information, consult *Helper applications* on page 68.

To save an inline image:

1. Navigate to the page that contains the image.

2. Right click the image and choose Save this Image as in the pop-up menu **(Figure 6.7)**. The Save As dialog box appears **(Figure 6.8)**.

3. Click OK to save the image with the name and extension given. The Saving Location dialog box shows you how long the download will take to finish **(Figure 6.9)**.

✔ Tips

■ Although you can change the extension of an image file when you save it, this will *not* magically change its format. To change an image's format, you need to use a program like Paintshop Pro or Adobe Photoshop.

■ You can also save an image by holding down the Shift key and clicking the image with the right mouse button.

■ If you click the Edit button while viewing a page with Netscape Gold, you *will* be allowed to save all the images it contains in one fell swoop *(see page 168)*.

Figure 6.7 *To save an inline image, right click the image and choose Save this Image as in the pop-up menu.*

Figure 6.8 *In the Save As dialog box, choose a file name (or use the existing one) and click OK.*

Figure 6.9 *The Saving Location dialog box shows how long it will take to download the image. You may continue browsing by clicking the main window.*

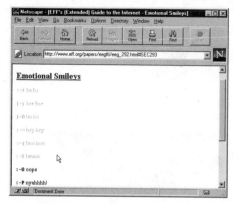

Figure 6.10 *Select (with the mouse) the part of the page that you wish to copy. Sometimes when you select, the text is shaded instead of highlighted (as shown here).*

Figure 6.11 *Choose Copy in the Edit menu.*

Figure 6.12 *Here I've pasted the copied material into a letter (in Word).*

Copying and pasting parts of a page

There is no law that says you must save an entire page when you are only interested in one portion of it. In addition, copying the page as described below is a fast and easy way to transfer information to other files in other applications.

To copy and paste part of a page:

1. With the mouse, select the part of the page that you wish to copy **(Figure 6.10)**.

2. Choose Copy in the Edit menu or press Ctrl+C **(Figure 6.11)**.

3. Place the cursor where you want to paste the material (perhaps in an e-mail note, in another application, or wherever).

4. Choose Paste in the Edit menu or press Ctrl+V. The text is pasted into the current window **(Figure 6.12)**.

✔ Tips

■ HTML tags and images cannot be copied using this technique. To save a page with HTML tags, consult *Saving a Web page* on page 54. To copy images, consult *Saving an image* on page 56.

■ You may not paste anything into an existing Web page in the Netscape browser. Of course, you may open a Web page (saved with HTML tags) with a word processor—or in Netscape Gold's Editor window *(see page 168)*—and then paste parts of other pages into it there.

Reading a saved page offline

If you've found an interesting but long page that you would like to read without hearing the connect-time clock ticking anxiously at your back, you can save the page, disconnect from your online service, and then open the page to read.

To read a saved page offline:

1. Save the page *with HTML tags* using the techniques described on page 54 or page 55.

2. Without quitting Netscape, disconnect from your online service.

3. From Netscape's File menu, choose Open File **(Figure 6.13)**. The Open dialog box appears.

4. Choose the file you saved in step 1 and click Open **(Figure 6.14)**. The page will appear in the Netscape browser **(Figure 6.15)**.

5. Read at your leisure.

✔ Tips

■ If you are saving several related pages for later reading, make sure to save them with their original names *(see page 55)*.

■ You can also view saved GIF or JPEG images offline. Simply choose the image in step 4 above. You may have to type the extension (*.gif or *.jpg) in the List Files of Type box. The image appears by itself in the browser.

■ If you saved the page in Plain Text format, it appears quite differently in the browser—without formatting, images or links **(Figure 6.16)**.

Figure 6.13 *To open a saved file, choose Open File in Netscape's File menu.*

Figure 6.14 *In the Open dialog box, choose the desired file and click Open.*

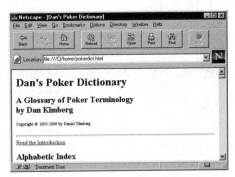

Figure 6.15 *The file (if saved as HTML Files—with HTML tags) appears with the original formatting and links, but without images.*

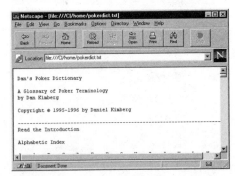

Figure 6.16 *If the file was saved as Plain Text (without HTML tags), it appears without formatting, links or images.*

Reading a saved page offline

Figure 6.17 *Navigate to the page that you want to print.*

Figure 6.18 *Choose Print in the File menu or click Print on the toolbar.*

Figure 6.19 *Choose Print Preview in the File menu before printing to see how the page will appear.*

Printing a page

You may want to create a hard copy of one of the pages that you find on the Web for future reference. Netscape automatically resizes the information on the Web page to fit on the printed page.

To print a page:

1. Navigate to the page that you wish to print **(Figure 6.17)**.

2. Choose Print in the File menu or click the Print button on the toolbar **(Figure 6.18)**. The standard Print dialog box appears.

3. If desired, change the printing options.

4. Click OK. The page will be printed.

✔ Tips

■ Printing an e-mail message, news posting or page that you are editing is practically identical to printing a Web page. Simply view the desired item and choose Print from the File menu.

■ Print an individual frame by clicking in the frame before choosing Print Frame in the File menu.

■ For more control on how the page is printed, consult *Setting up printing options* on page 60.

■ Choose Print Preview in the File menu **(Figure 6.19)** before printing to get an idea on screen of how the page will look when printed.

Printing a page

Setting up printing options

When you print a page, you can decide whether to include a header or footer, what margins to use, whether certain elements should appear in black or in color, and what order the pages should print in.

Figure 6.20 *Choose Page Setup in the File menu.*

To set the printing options:

1. Choose Page Setup in the File menu **(Figure 6.20)**. The Page Setup dialog box appears **(Figure 6.21)**.

2. In the Page Options section, unmark Beveled Lines to simplify beveled frames in tables and around images. Choose Black Text and Black lines to print horizontal lines without shading or color. Choose Last Page First to reverse the printing order.

Figure 6.21 *In the Page Setup Options dialog box, adjust how graphic elements should print, the width of the margins, and the contents of the header and footer.*

3. In the Margins section, enter the amount of space for the margins.

4. In the Header section, check Document Title to print the page's title at the top of each page. Check Document Location (URL) to print the page's URL at the top of each page.

5. In the Footer section, check Page Number to add the page number to the bottom of each page. Check Page Total to print the total number of pages at the bottom of each page. Check Date Printed to print the current date at the bottom of each page.

6. Click OK to save the options.

✔ Tip

■ The options in the Page Setup dialog box affect all the pages you print from that moment onwards, not just the current document.

Setting up printing options

Finding Stuff on the Web

Figure 7.1 *Type two words that you wish to search for, separated by a space, in Netscape's Location field.*

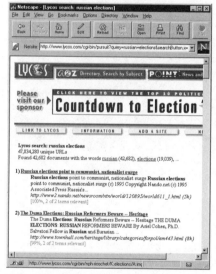

Figure 7.2 *Netscape connects to any one of a number of search services and enters your criteria. The search service returns a list of possible matches. (This is Lycos.)*

With millions of Web pages, fourteen thousand newsgroups, and countless e-mail users, it is sometimes a challenge to find the information that you're looking for. There are many companies that offer Internet search services in exchange for a glance at their advertisers' promotions.

There are services that search Web pages, services that search newsgroups, services that search for e-mail addresses and even services that catalog shareware. You simply jump to the service that is most likely to have the information you need.

Using Netscape to search

Another improvement in Netscape 3 is that you can access search services automatically (if randomly), just by entering the criteria in the Location field.

To search with Netscape:

1. In the Location field, type two or more words that you wish to search for separated with a space **(Fig. 7.1)**.

2. Press Enter. Netscape connects to one of several search services (like those described in this chapter) and enters your search criteria. A list of possible matches appears **(Figure 7.2)**.

✔ Tips

- To search for only one word, simply type it twice, separated by a space.

- If you're not satisfied with the results, do it over. Netscape almost never uses the same search engine twice in a row.

Using Netscape to search

Finding Web pages by subject

One of the best known Web page search indexes is Yahoo!. Yahoo! sorts its Web index by topic, and creates a kind of Table of Contents for the Web. If you want to see several pages about the same or related general topics, or if you just want a place to start surfing, Yahoo! is a good place to begin.

To use Yahoo! to find Web pages by topic:

1. Choose Open Location in the File menu or click the Open button on the toolbar **(Figure 7.3)**. The Open Location dialog box appears **(Figure 7.4)**.

2. Type Yahoo!'s URL address (or simply type **yahoo**) in the text box and click Open. Netscape displays the Yahoo! home page **(Figure 7.5)**. Each main topic is divided into clickable subtopics.

3. Click any topic or subtopic of interest. Yahoo! displays a set of related links **(Figure 7.6)**. The links may be divided into indices (lists of related links), subtopics (which when clicked on reveal a list of links to pages about the subtopic) or Web pages (that fit the general topic but none of the subtopics listed).

4. Click the desired link. The page is displayed **(Figure 7.7)**.

✔ Tip

■ You can also search for keywords through Yahoo! by entering the words in the text box and clicking Search. However, there are other services that are better at straight word searches.

Figure 7.3 *Choose Open Location in the File menu (left) or click the Open button (right).*

Figure 7.4 *Type Yahoo's URL address in the dialog box and click Open.*

Figure 7.5 *The Yahoo! home page is divided into categories and subcategories, all of which are links to related articles.*

Finding Web pages by subject

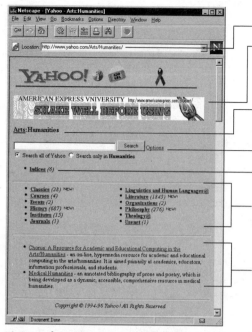

Yahoo's address is displayed in the Location text box.

Advertisements are sprinkled liberally throughout the Yahoo! site. This is how Yahoo! makes money, but you don't have to pay attention.

Yahoo! always lists the path that you have taken. You can click on the links to the earlier pages to go back (up) in the hierarchy of categories.

You can also choose to search for a keyword, either in the entire Yahoo! index, or just in the pages that are in the currently selected category.

The Indices are pages that contain a collection of links to the main topic (Humanities, in this case).

Yahoo! divides all the articles into subcategories. The number after each category indicates how many articles it contains. An @ symbol means that the subcategory is further divided into smaller subcategories.

The articles that are general enough to be related to the main category (Humanities) but that don't fit into any subcategories, are listed at the bottom of the page.

Figure 7.6 *A click on Humanities brings up this page of related links, divided into subcategories.*

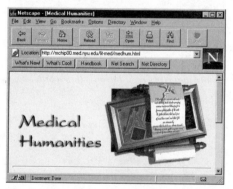

Figure 7.7 *A click on a link in Figure 7.6 brings you to the corresponding article out on the Web. You are no longer at the Yahoo! site.*

Searching for Web pages by keyword

There are two or three good search services that have indexed as much of the Web as they can find—by sending out automatic robots called *spiders* that go from server to server looking at all the Web pages and recording their addresses, titles and sometimes even their contents. One comprehensive service I've found is Altavista (by Digital), that claims to include some 30 million pages in its index.

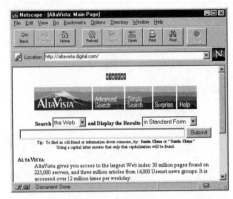

Figure 7.8 *Altavista's home page.*

To search for Web pages by keyword with Altavista:

1. Choose Open Location or click the Open button on the toolbar. The Open Location dialog box appears.

2. Type **altavista.digital.com** in the text box and click Open. Netscape displays the Altavista home page **(Figure 7.8)**.

3. Type a word or phrase in the text box **(Figure 7.9)**.

Figure 7.9 *Type the criteria (first, cosmos, and then, flowers). Use plus signs before the words to ensure that every page includes that word.*

4. Choose where you wish Altavista to search in the left pop-up menu. Choose The Web for Web pages and Usenet for newsgroup articles.

5. Choose how results should be displayed (Standard, Compact or Detailed) in the right pop-up menu.

6. Click Submit to start the search. Altavista shows the links to the pages that satisfied the search criteria **(Fig. 7.10)**.

7. If desired, click Next or the page numbers to see more matches.

8. Click on one of the links to display the corresponding page **(Figure 7.11)**.

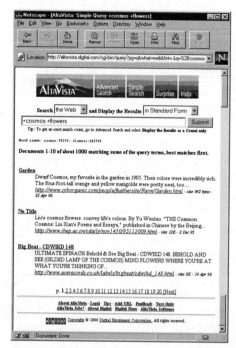

Figure 7.10 *Altavista lists the pages that meet the criteria. Click on a page to jump to it. Click on Next or on a particular page number to see that page of links.*

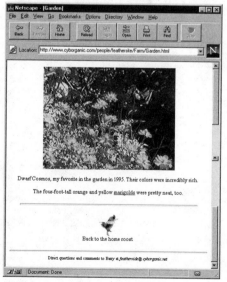

Figure 7.11 *The desired page is shown in the browser.*

✔ **Tips**

■ Make sure you spell the keyword(s) correctly. If you type "Catchmear" when looking for lush, goat fiber, you are likely to be disappointed.

■ Precede words that *must* appear on the page with a plus sign (+) and words that you wish to *exclude* with a minus sign (-).

■ Use the asterisk (*) as a wild card to find alternate spellings. For example, type **theat*** to find both *theater* and *theatre*.

■ Search for a contiguous phrase in a page by inserting the words in double quotes: **"The New York Times"**.

■ Use upper case letters to restrict the search to words with those upper case letters. Lower case letters are case-insensitive. (**Frank** finds only *Frank*; **frank** finds both *Frank* and *frank*.)

■ To find pages with links to *your* page, type **link:url**, replacing *url* with the URL of your page. To omit links from your own pages, add **-url:yoursite**.

■ In Altavista's advanced query area, you can use operators like Near to find people like Ronnie Schwartz (type Ronnie NEAR Schwartz).

■ Lycos (*http://www.lycos.com*), Excite (*http://www.excite.com*), and Open Text (*http://www.opentext.com/omw/f-omw.html*) are three other word-based Web search services.

■ Review Altavista's Tips and Help pages (click on the Tips or Help buttons) to get more information on refined searches.

Searching for Web pages by keyword

Searching for people and organizations

Remember Ronnie Schwartz from college? Haven't talked to him lately? Maybe you can find him. Although there's no centralized white pages (at least not for free), there are services that attempt to track down and index e-mail addresses.

To search for a person's e-mail address:

1. Choose Open Location or click the Open button on the toolbar.

2. Type **whowhere** in the text box and click Open to display the WhoWhere? home page. You can search by person or by organization.

3. If you're looking for a person, type the person's name in the text box in the middle frame **(Fig. 7.12)**.

4. If desired, scroll down to enter information about the person's organization or location.

5. Click the Search button—you may have to scroll down in the middle frame to find it **(Figure 7.13)**. WhoWhere? displays the results as links, and divides them into three categories: highly, probably, and possibly relevant **(Figure 7.14)**.

✔ Tips

■ Click on a person's address to send her an e-mail message right away.

■ To save an address, press the right mouse button and select Copy this Link Location in the submenu. Save the address as described on page 132.

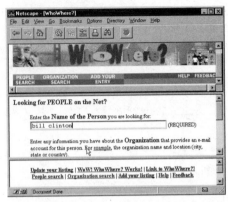

Figure 7.12 *In the middle frame, enter the name of the person whose e-mail address you want to find.*

Figure 7.13 *Scroll down in the middle frame to find the Search button and click it.*

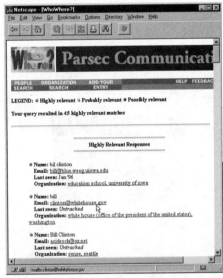

Figure 7.14 *Scroll through the list of matches to see if the person you were looking for is there. Click the name to send an e-mail message.*

Figure 7.15 *Click Organization Search in the top frame of the WhoWhere? home page.*

Figure 7.16 *Type the name of the organization in the text box in the middle frame and click Search.*

Figure 7.17 *In the list that appears, click the organization that you were looking for.*

Figure 7.18 *Once you click the link to the organization, Netscape shows its home page (in this case, Warner Brothers' home page).*

You can also use WhoWhere? to look for an organizations' Web site. Although many organizations have guessable URLs in the form of *www.organization.com*, others do not. WhoWhere? bridges the gap.

To find an organization:

1. Follow steps 1 and 2 on the previous page.

2. Click Organization Search in the top frame of the WhoWhere? home page **(Figure 7.15)**.

3. Type the name of the organization, and if desired, its location (city or state) in the text box **(Figure 7.16)**.

4. Click the Search button or press Return. WhoWhere? shows you the links to the pages that satisfy the search criteria **(Figure 7.17)**.

5. Click on the desired link. (Links to organizations tend to be Web pages as opposed to e-mail addresses.) The newly found page is displayed **(Figure 7.18)**.

✔ Tip

■ Before doing a search, try typing **www.organization.com** in the Open Location dialog box or in the Location field, where *organization* is the name of the company you're looking for. Theoretically, you could just type **organization** *(see page 26)* but I've had better luck typing the whole thing. If the name has a space (like Warner Brothers), you'll have to search for the proper address, since URLs cannot contain a space.

Finding an article in a newsgroup

There are over 14,000 newsgroups, and each of them receives from several to several hundred messages a day. Finding a message that deals with a particular topic can be difficult. You can use Deja News to search for newsgroup messages.

To do a quick search for an article in a newsgroup:

1. Choose Open Location or click the Open button on the toolbar.

2. Type **dejanews** in the text box and click Open.

3. In the Deja News home page that appears, type the search criteria, and click the Find button **(Figure 7.19)**.

4. Deja News lists the articles that fit the criteria **(Figure 7.20)**. Click an article that interests you to view that message. The message is shown in the browser, not the News window **(Figure 7.21)**.

5. If desired, you can reply to the posting by clicking Post Article. You'll be automatically switched to the News window. Or, e-mail a response to the writer by clicking Email Reply. A regular Message Composition window will appear.

✔ Tips

■ You can also refine requests further by clicking Power Search at the top of Deja News' home page.

■ You can also use Altavista (see page 64) to search for newsgroup articles.

Figure 7.19 *In Deja News' home page, type the keywords and click Find.*

Figure 7.20 *Deja News shows the news postings that match your request. Click one to view it.*

Figure 7.21 *The news posting appears in the browser window. To reply, click Post Article or Email Reply*

Figure 7.22 *Click Search to get to this main Search window, then choose the appropriate platform, the keywords (in this example, After Dark), the number of files you wish to display and an optional second keyword. Click Start search.*

Figure 7.23 *The shareware programs or updates that satisfy the criteria given in the Search window (Figure 7.22) are listed in the central frame. Click one to see the available FTP sites.*

Figure 7.24 *When you click a file to download, shareware.com lists the FTP sites where you can find it. Click an FTP site to download the file.*

Finding shareware through the Web

Sometimes, the hardest part about downloading a file is finding it. One service that provides you with the FTP addresses for over 160,000 shareware programs (as well as commercial software updates) is shareware.com by C/net.

To find shareware through the Web:

1. Choose Open Location or click the Open button on the toolbar.

2. Type **shareware** in the text box and click Open. The C/net home page appears.

3. Click Search in either the left or top right frame to begin **(Figure 7.22)**.

4. Choose the desired platform in the Select platform submenu.

5. Type the appropriate keywords in the Search word submenu.

6. If desired, type a second key word and select And or Or.

7. Click Start search. The shareware files that satisfy the criteria given are listed in the central frame **(Figure 7.23)**.

8. Click the desired file to list the FTP sites where it can be found as well as its approximate download time **(Figure 7.24)**.

9. Click the desired FTP site to download the file. For more information on FTP transfers, consult *Downloading files* on page 50.

Finding information in an open page

You've been reading this whole chapter thinking to yourself, "Hah, I know an easier way. What about the Find button on the toolbar?" The problem with the Find button is that it only searches within a particular page (or message or post). It doesn't search out on the Web. So, if you're looking for a particular word or phrase within a long document that you're already viewing, that's when you should use the Find button.

To find information in an open page:

1. Jump to the desired page.

2. Click the Find button on the toolbar **(Figure 7.25)** or choose Find in the Edit menu **(Figure 7.26)**. The Find dialog box appears.

3. Type the word or phrase that you wish to look for and click Find Next **(Figure 7.27)**. Netscape will highlight the first occurrence of the word, if any, in the currently open page **(Figure 7.28)**.

4. If desired, choose Find Next in the dialog box (if it's showing) to find the next occurrence of the search word or phrase. If the Find dialog box is not showing, choose Find Next in the Edit menu.

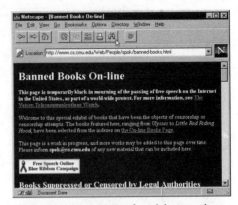

Figure 7.25 *Once you've found the page that contains the information, click the Find button to jump to the desired text.*

Figure 7.26 *You can also choose Find in the Edit menu.*

Figure 7.27 *Type the text you're looking for and click Find Next.*

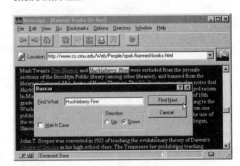

Figure 7.28 *Netscape highlights the found text. If this is the text you want, click on the page to make the browser active. If it's not, click Find Next to find the next occurrence.*

Figure 7.29 *Choose Netscape's Home in the Directory menu to jump to Netscape's home page.*

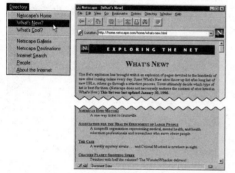

Figure 7.30 *Choose What's New? to see which sites Netscape has discovered lately.*

Figure 7.31 *Choose What's Cool? in the Directory menu to see what Netscape Corporations considers a "cool" page.*

Figure 7.32 *You can also choose What's New? and What's Cool? (among other things) with the Directory buttons. Personally, I think they just take up much needed window space. To hide them, consult Controlling a browser's appearance on page 19.*

Checking out Netscape's pages

Some of Netscape's menu commands take you to particular pages on the Web (mostly on Netscape's own site). Some of these sites are kind of helpful. Some are less so.

To find Netscape's home page:

Choose Netscape's Home in the Directory menu (**Figure 7.29**) or click the Netscape icon at the right side of the browser.

To find new pages (according to Netscape):

Choose What's New? in the Directory menu or click the What's New? button at the top of the browser (**Figure 7.30 and Figure 7.32**).

To find cool pages (according to Netscape):

Choose What's Cool? in the Directory menu or click the What's Cool? button at the top of the browser (**Figure 7.31 and Figure 7.32**).

To find servers built with Netscape servers software:

Choose Netscape Galleria in the Directory menu.

To search the Web with Netscape's search service:

Choose Netscape Destinations, Internet Search, or People in the Directory menu. (For more information on finding Web pages, read the rest of this chapter.)

Checking out Netscape's pages

Finding Netscape documentation

A couple of Netscape's built-in commands link you to help pages, including the documentation for Netscape itself.

To find the Netscape handbook:

Choose Handbook in the Help menu **(Figure 7.33)**. Netscape's documentation will be displayed **(Figure 7.34)**. This is the same documentation you would get if you bought the manuals—although perhaps more up-to-date.

FAQ, which rhymes with *smack* and stands for Frequently Asked Questions, is a list of questions that Netscape has received over and over again. Your question may or may not be among them. Answers are included.

To find the Netscape FAQ:

1. Choose Frequently Asked Questions in the Help menu **(Figure 7.35)**.

2. Click the Netscape Navigator FAQ link **(Figure 7.36)**. Netscape's FAQs on Navigator are divided into several files.

3. Click on the FAQ link that interests you.

✔ Tip

■ One more good source for help on specific Netscape functions is the Help button you'll find in many dialog boxes. Click it to access Netscape's Help file.

Figure 7.33 *Choose Handbook in the Help menu to view the Netscape documentation.*

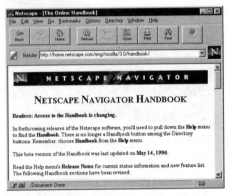

Figure 7.34 *The Handbook page has the advantage of always being the latest version available.*

Figure 7.35 *Choose Frequently Asked Questions in the Help menu.*

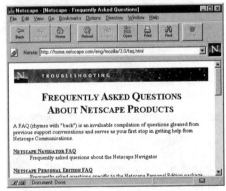

Figure 7.36 *Click the Netscape Navigator FAQ link to see if your question has already been answered in Netscape's files, in which you case you'll be able to quickly find a response.*

Figure 7.37 *Choose Open Location in the File menu (or click the Open button on the toolbar).*

Figure 7.38 *Type the URL address for the support request form in the Open Location box.*

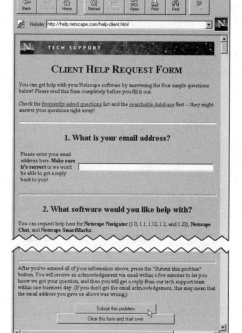

Figure 7.39 *Fill out the Client Help Request Form (it's long) and then click the Submit this problem button at the bottom of the page.*

Finding technical support

Netscape offers free technical support by telephone to users who have bought the Personal Edition of Netscape Navigator, or for users who have downloaded the LAN version by modem and then registered and paid for it. If you have not paid for Netscape, they will charge you $25 for the first 15 minutes, plus $2 for each additional minute.

To find technical support by telephone:

Call 1-800-320-2099. Press 1 for automated support and 2 to wait for an operator.

Only registered LAN version Netscape users can get support via e-mail.

To send a message to Netscape technical support:

1. Choose Open Location in the File menu **(Figure 7.37)** or click the Open button. The Open Location dialog box appears **(Figure 7.38)**.

2. Type **http://help.netscape.com/ help-client.html**.

3. Fill out the form.

4. Click Submit this problem at the bottom of the page **(Figure 7.39)**. As long as you are a registered LAN version Netscape user, you should receive a notification in a couple of hours and a response within a few days.

✔ Tip

■ If you choose How to Get Support from the Help menu, you'll get referred to the handbook and the FAQs before you finally reach the form shown in Figure 7.39.

Finding info about your Netscape software

Netscape's menus offer ways to get information about the software itself. You can find out what version you have, what plug-ins you have installed, what your registration number is, what upgrade options you have, and what new features have been added to the program since your version was released.

To get information about your Netscape software:

1. Choose About Netscape in the Help menu. The version number of your software is displayed **(Figure 7.40)**.

2. Click in the Netscape logo (in the About Netscape page) to see information about the software engineers who developed Netscape.

3. Choose About Plug-ins in the Help menu. A list of the currently installed plug-ins is displayed **(Figure 7.41)**.

4. Choose Registration Information in the Help menu. Your registration number is displayed **(Figure 7.42)**. If you have not yet registered your copy of Netscape, information on how to register will be shown.

5. Choose Software in the Help menu. Netscape displays its upgrades page **(Figure 7.43)**.

6. Choose Release Notes in the Help menu. A list of the new features included in your copy of Netscape appears **(Figure 7.44)**.

Figure 7.40 *Choose About Netscape in the Help menu to see what version you are using.*

Figure 7.41 *Choose About Plug-ins in the Help menu to see which plug-ins you have installed.*

Figure 7.42 *Choose Registration Information to see your registration ID.*

Figure 7.43 *Choose Software in the Help menu to see what upgrade options you have.*

Figure 7.44 *Choose Release Notes to see a list of new features for your version of Netscape.*

Bookmarks

Figure 8.1 *The Bookmarks window helps you organize your favorite sites and get back to them with a simple double click.*

Figure 8.2 *The Bookmarks menu in the main Netscape window lets you navigate to your favorite sites without pulling up the Bookmarks window.*

Figure 8.3 *Choose Bookmarks in the Window menu to open the Bookmarks window.*

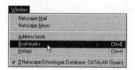

Figure 8.4 *Or choose Go to Bookmarks in the Bookmarks menu to open the Bookmarks window.*

What is a bookmark?

There are approximately 4 million Web pages already in existence. If someday you should find a link to a gem of a page, you won't want to lose it. With Netscape you can store the URL addresses to your favorite sites as *bookmarks*. The next time you want to jump to that site, instead of trying to remember the circuitous route you took the first time, simply pull up your Bookmarks window **(Figure 8.1)**, double click and sail in. Or surf. Whatever.

The bookmarks that you create are listed in the Bookmarks window, which you can display on screen or hide at your convenience. They are also listed at the bottom of the Bookmarks menu for easy access **(Figure 8.2)**.

To open the Bookmarks window:

Choose Bookmarks in the Window menu **(Figure 8.3)** or choose Go to Bookmarks in the Bookmarks menu **(Figure 8.4)**. The Bookmarks window appears.

Using bookmarks to navigate the Web

Bookmarks make it easy to find your way back to favorite sites. The truth is, typing URLs is a pain. It's easy to mix up lower and upper case letters, leave off a forward slash, or simply misspell part of the address. Navigating with bookmarks is a breeze—double click and you're there.

To navigate with the Bookmarks window:

1. Choose Bookmarks in the Window menu. The Bookmarks window appears.

2. Double click a bookmark to jump to the corresponding Web page. You may also click once on a bookmark and choose Go to Bookmark in the Item menu **(Figure 8.5)**. The page is displayed in the browser **(Figure 8.7)**.

To navigate with the Bookmarks menu:

1. Choose the desired Web page from the Bookmarks menu in the main Netscape window **(Figure 8.6)**. The page is displayed in the browser **(Figure 8.7)**.

✔ Tip

■ Double click a folder in the Bookmarks window to open it and see its contents or to close it and hide its contents. You can tell that a folder is open by the icon of an open folder and by the symbol to its left. A plus sign indicates a closed folder while a minus sign indicates an open folder.

Figure 8.5 *Select a bookmark and choose Go to Bookmark or double click a bookmark to go to the corresponding page on the Web.*

Figure 8.6 *If you don't have the Bookmarks window open, it may be faster to use the Bookmarks menu. Simply select the page desired to jump to it.*

Figure 8.7 *The chosen page is displayed in the browser.*

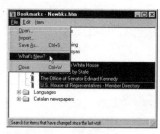

Figure 8.8 *Choose What's New? in the Bookmarks window's File menu. Here we've selected a few bookmarks to check.*

Figure 8.9 *Check All bookmarks to search the entire file or Selected Bookmarks to search the selected bookmarks. Choose Start Checking.*

Figure 8.10 *A dialog appears in which you can watch Netscape's progress, or click Cancel if you get impatient.*

Figure 8.11 *Netscape marks changed pages with "bright" marks (all but the first bookmark in the selection). A question mark means the program can't tell if there have been changes or not (as in the* Welcome to the White House *bookmark).*

Checking what's new

Netscape can look through all your bookmarks, or through a selected group of them, and tell which pages have been changed or updated since your last visit.

To check what's new:

1. If desired, choose the bookmarks that you wish to check.

2. Choose What's New? in the Bookmarks window's File menu **(Fig. 8.8)**. The What's New? dialog box appears.

3. If you made a selection of bookmarks, click Selected Bookmarks **(Fig. 8.9)**. Otherwise, leave All Bookmarks checked. Click OK. Netscape connects to each of the pages listed in your bookmarks file to see if they've changed since your last visit.

4. A dialog box appears that charts Netscape's progress **(Figure 8.10)**. Click Cancel if you get tired of waiting. Netscape gives you a final report. Then Netscape displays changed bookmarks with "bright" marks **(Figure 8.11)**. Bookmarks that Netscape was unable to analyze are indicated with a question mark.

✔ Tip

■ When you create a bookmark manually, Netscape marks it with a question mark, indicating that you have not visited it.

Setting the New Bookmarks folder

When you add a bookmark, it is automatically appended to the New Bookmarks folder in the current bookmarks file. By default, Netscape sets up the principal folder to receive new bookmarks. However, you can choose any folder as the receiving folder, making it easy to add several bookmarks at a time to a particular category.

To set the New Bookmarks folder:

1. Click once on the folder to which new bookmarks should be added when you use the Add Bookmark command in the Bookmarks menu. You may choose any folder at any level in the Bookmarks window.

2. Choose Set to New Bookmarks Folder in the Item menu in the Bookmarks window **(Figure 8.12)**. The new New Bookmarks folder is indicated by a folder with the bookmark icon inside it **(Figure 8.13)**.

Figure 8.12 *Choose the folder that you want to add new bookmarks to and then choose Set to New Bookmarks Folder in the Item menu (in the Bookmarks window).*

Figure 8.13 *A bookmark icon appears in the folder that you have designated as the "New Bookmarks folder".*

Figure 8.14 *To select the folder from which the Bookmarks menu will be generated, click the folder to select it, and then choose Set to Bookmark Menu Folder in the Item menu (in the Bookmarks window).*

Figure 8.15 *The new "Bookmarks Menu folder" has a menu icon on top of the folder icon.*

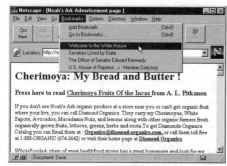

Figure 8.16 *The Bookmarks menu shows only those bookmarks that are contained in the folder that you've designated as the "Bookmarks Menu Folder".*

Setting the Bookmarks menu folder

The Bookmarks menu is generated from the bookmarks in the Bookmarks window in order to give you rapid access to your bookmarks. You can choose which folder in the Bookmarks window is used to create the menu.

To set the Bookmarks menu folder:

1. Click once on the folder from which you want to generate the Bookmarks menu. You can choose any folder at any level of the Bookmarks window.

2. Choose Set to Bookmark Menu Folder in the Item menu in the Bookmarks window **(Figure 8.14)**. A menu icon appears on top of the folder icon **(Figure 8.15)**.

3. Display the Bookmarks menu to see the new configuration **(Figure 8.16)**.

✔ **Harrumph**

■ OK, this isn't really a tip, just a complaint. The menu is called "Bookmarks" not "Bookmark" so why is the option called "Set to Bookmark Menu Folder"? Ask Netscape.

Setting the Bookmarks menu folder

Adding a bookmark from a Web site

The hardest part about creating a bookmark is finding a page that is worth going back to. Once you are there, adding a reference to the page is a snap.

To add a bookmark:

1. Navigate to the page whose URL you wish to save.

2. Choose Add Bookmark in the Bookmarks menu **(Figure 8.17)**. The title and URL of the Web page that you are currently browsing will be saved in a bookmark in the New Bookmarks folder *(see page 78)* and will be automatically appended to the Bookmarks menu **(Figure 8.18)**.

✔ Tips

■ You can also drag links from a page (or mail message or news posting) to the Bookmarks window.

■ Drag the chain link icon to the Bookmarks window to add a link to the current page.

■ Right click a link and then choose Add Bookmark for this Link in the pop-up menu to add a link from a page without going to the page.

■ When you add a link by dragging or choosing Add Bookmark for this Link in the pop-up menu, the URL (and not the title of the page) is used as the bookmark title. For information on changing the bookmark's title, consult *Editing a bookmark or folder* on page 84.

Figure 8.17 *Once you have found a good page, simply choose Add Bookmark (Ctrl+D) from the Bookmarks menu to add the page to your bookmarks file.*

Figure 8.18
The current page's title and URL are immediately added to the Bookmarks menu (as shown) and to the Bookmarks window.

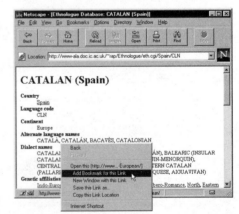

Figure 8.19 *Right click the link and choose Add Bookmark for this Link in the pop-up menu.*

Adding a bookmark from a Web site

Figure 8.20 *Choose Insert Bookmark in the Item menu (in the Bookmarks window) to open the Bookmark Properties dialog box.*

Figure 8.21 *The Bookmark Properties dialog box contains information about the Title, URL and Location of a bookmark. You may edit a bookmark at any time by opening this dialog box.*

Figure 8.22 *The new bookmark appears in the Bookmarks window with a question mark next to it. The question mark means the bookmark has not yet been visited.*

Adding a bookmark by hand

You don't need to connect to a page in order to add it to your bookmark file. As long as you know a page's URL—perhaps you've found a reference in a magazine—you can create a bookmark for the page manually.

Adding a bookmark by hand:

1. Open the Bookmarks window by choosing Bookmarks in the Window menu. The Bookmarks window appears.

2. Choose Insert Bookmark in the Item menu (in the Bookmarks window) **(Figure 8.20)**. The Bookmark Properties dialog box appears **(Fig. 8.21)**.

3. Type a title for the new bookmark in the Name text box. This title will appear in the Go menu and in the Bookmarks window.

4. Type (or copy) the URL for the page in the Location (URL) text box.

5. Finally, if desired, enter a short description of the page in the Description text box.

6. Click OK to add the bookmark to your bookmarks file **(Figure 8.22)**.

✔ Tips

■ Type upper and lower case letters in URLs exactly as they were, and beware of typos.

■ You can add bookmarks manually without connecting to the Internet thereby saving connect time and phone charges.

Creating aliases of bookmarks

An alias is a sort of remote control. You can create aliases of your bookmarks in order to have access to your favorite sites in several locations in your bookmarks file. You use an alias exactly the same way you use a regular bookmark. The big difference is that if you change the URL or description of the original bookmark, the corresponding aliases are updated automatically.

To create an alias:

1. Click once on the bookmark that you wish to create an alias of.

2. Choose Make Alias in the Item menu in the Bookmarks menu **(Fig. 8.23)**. The alias appears below the original bookmark **(Figure 8.24)**. If you open the Properties window of an alias, its URL is blank, since it depends on the URL of the parent bookmark.

3. Drag the alias to the new location **(Figure 8.25)**.

4. If desired, edit the alias to give it a new name or description. For more information, consult *Editing a bookmark or folder* on page 84.

✔ Tips

■ You may not edit an alias' URL, since it comes directly from the bookmark. To change an alias' URL, change the URL of the *source* bookmark.

■ If you change a bookmark's description, you won't see the change in the alias' Bookmark Properties dialog box. However, if you open the bookmarks file as a Web page *(see page 89)*, the description will be updated correctly.

Figure 8.23
After selecting the source bookmark, choose Make Alias in the Item menu (in the Bookmarks window).

Figure 8.24 *The alias is created and placed below the selected bookmark. The alias appears identical to the original.*

Figure 8.25
Drag the new alias to another folder so that you can access the corresponding page from more than one place.

Figure 8.26 *To create a new folder for organizing your bookmarks, choose Insert Folder in the Item menu.*

Figure 8.27 *Use the Bookmark Properties window to change the Name and Description of folders as well as bookmarks. You cannot associate a URL with a folder. (It wouldn't make sense anyway.)*

Figure 8.28 *The new folder appears directly below (and inside) the selected one.*

Creating a bookmark folder

If you have a lot of bookmarks, sooner or later you will find that searching through your list is almost as troublesome as searching through the Web. The solution is a little organization. You can categorize your bookmarks and separate them into named folders.

To create a bookmark folder:

1. Open the Bookmarks window by choosing Bookmarks in the Window menu. The Bookmarks window appears. If you haven't created any folders yet, all the bookmarks will be in the default folder that Netscape creates for you.

2. Select the folder in which you wish to create the new folder.

3. Choose Insert Folder in the Item menu in the Bookmarks window **(Figure 8.26)**. The Bookmark Properties dialog box appears **(Fig. 8.27)**.

4. In the Name field, type the name for your new folder.

5. In the Description field, enter a few words that define your category. This is a good way to help you remember what goes in this folder which, in turn, makes the folder more useful.

6. Click OK. The new folder appears in the Bookmarks window, below—that is, *inside*—the selected folder **(Figure 8.28)**.

7. Drag bookmarks or other folders to the new folder.

Creating a bookmark folder

Editing a bookmark or folder

When you add a bookmark with the Add Bookmark command, the title of the page is automatically used in the Bookmarks window to identify the bookmark. You may wish to give the bookmark a name that more clearly identifies its contents. In addition, you can change a bookmark's URL (perhaps, the creators of the page have moved it to a new server) or change its description.

To edit a bookmark:

1. Open the Bookmarks window by choosing Bookmarks in the Window menu. The Bookmarks window appears.

2. Click once on the bookmark that you wish to edit. Choose Properties in the Item menu (in the Bookmarks window) **(Figure 8.29)**. The Bookmark Properties dialog box appears **(Figure 8.30)**.

3. Change the Name, URL, and Description in the corresponding text boxes as desired **(Figure 8.31)**.

4. Click OK to save the changes. The bookmark's information is automatically updated in the Bookmarks window.

✔ Tip

■ To delete a bookmark or folder (or separator) that you don't use anymore, select it and choose Delete in the Edit menu **(Figure 8.32)** or press Delete (not Backspace).

Figure 8.29 *Choose the Properties command in the Item menu to display the Bookmark Properties window.*

Figure 8.30 *In the Bookmark Properties window, you may change the Title to better identify the page's contents, update a page's URL, or add a description for the page.*

Figure 8.31 *Once you click OK to save the changes, the new data is automatically updated in the Bookmarks window and Bookmarks menu.*

Figure 8.32 *To delete a bookmark, select it and then choose Delete from the Edit menu (in the Bookmarks window). You can also select the bookmark and then press the Delete key.*

Figure 8.33 *To add a separator, first select the bookmark or folder below which you wish to insert the separator. Choose Insert Separator in the Item menu in the Bookmarks window.*

Figure 8.34 *The separator appears below the currently selected item. You may insert separators at any level of the Bookmarks hierarchy.*

Figure 8.35 *The separator appears as a gray line in the Bookmarks menu.*

Adding a separator

If you have several folders, it may be helpful to have a visual clue that separates them. Since the Bookmarks menu is generated from your Bookmarks window, the separators that you include in the window will also appear in the menu.

To add a separator to your bookmarks window:

1. Click once on the folder or bookmark directly above the place where you wish to insert a separator.

2. Choose Insert Separator in the Item menu in the Bookmarks window **(Figure 8.33)**. A bookmark icon appears in the desired location with the word *<separator>* to its right **(Figure 8.34)**.

3. Click on the Bookmarks menu to see your new separator **(Figure 8.34)**.

✔ Tip

■ You are not limited to adding separators only between folders. You can insert a separator between any two objects in the Bookmarks window, regardless of their levels.

Sorting your bookmarks file

If you have more than five or six bookmarks in a folder, or more than five or six
folders in your bookmarks file, you may
wish to alphabetize the items to make
them easier to find.

To sort your bookmarks:

Choose Sort Bookmarks in the Item menu
(Figure 8.36). All of the folders and
bookmarks will be sorted alphabetically
(Figure 8.37). Separators are placed at
the top of the list. Thankfully, the hierarchy is maintained.

✔ Tip

■ You can undo a sort; simply choose
Undo in the Edit menu. (Be sure you
choose the Undo command in the
Bookmarks window's Edit menu and
not the browser's Edit menu.)

Figure 8.36 *Choose Sort
Bookmarks in the Item menu
(in the Bookmarks window).*

Figure 8.37 *The bookmarks are sorted alphabetically, in descending order.*

Sorting your bookmarks file

Figure 8.38 *To save a bookmarks file, perhaps to share it with friends or as a backup, choose Save As in the File menu in the Bookmarks window.*

Figure 8.39 *In the Save bookmarks file dialog box, type the name for the new bookmarks file, and choose HTML Files in the Save Files as Type pop-up menu. Then click Save.*

Saving a bookmarks file

You can save a bookmarks file to give to friends, or simply to make a back-up copy. In fact, a bookmarks file is nothing more than an HTML page that you can browse as you would any other local file.

To save a bookmark file:

1. Choose Save As in the File menu in the Bookmarks window **(Figure 8.38)**. A standard Save As dialog box appears **(Figure 8.39)**.

2. Give the file a name and choose the directory in which to save it.

3. Choose a file type for the bookmarks file. If you want to open the file with Netscape, choose HTML Files. To open the file in a word processor or text editor, choose Plain Text (*.txt).

4. Click Save to save the file.

✔ Tips

■ If you choose HTML Files when saving the bookmark file, Netscape automatically tacks the extension .htm to the end of the bookmark file's name so that you'll be able to open the file as a regular Web page *(see page 89)*.

■ For example, if the bookmarks file has the proper extension (.htm), you'll be able to designate it as your home page. This way, each time you open Netscape, you will have your favorite sites just a click away. For more information, consult *Choosing a home page* on page 17.

Opening a different bookmarks file

Although your bookmarks file is hidden from view when you close the Bookmarks window, it is not gone. Simply open the window again to see the bookmarks file again. If, however, you wish to open a *different* bookmarks file, you must follow these steps.

To open a different bookmarks file:

1. Open the Bookmarks window by choosing Bookmarks in the Window menu.

2. Choose Open in the File menu of the Bookmarks window **(Figure 8.40)**. A standard Open dialog box appears **(Figure 8.41)**.

3. Navigate to the bookmarks file that you wish to open, and double click it to open it. The new bookmarks file will replace the current one in the Bookmarks window **(Figure 8.42)**. The old bookmarks file will remain intact in its former location.

✔ Tip

■ Saving and opening multiple bookmarks files is an ideal way to share links to cool pages. Since the bookmarks file is nothing more than a simple HTML file, you can also open it directly with Netscape—on PCs, Macs or even Unix machines—no matter what kind of computer the bookmark file comes from. *(See "Opening a bookmarks file as a Web page" on page 89.)*

Figure 8.40
To open a different bookmarks file, choose Open in the File menu in the Bookmarks window.

Figure 8.41 *In the standard Open dialog box that appears, choose the bookmarks file that you want to open.*

Figure 8.42 *The bookmarks in the new bookmarks file that you've just opened replace the ones from the old bookmarks file. The old bookmarks file remains intact on your disk.*

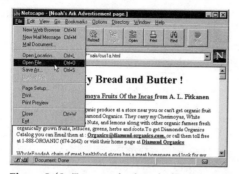

Figure 8.43 *To open a bookmarks file as a Web page, choose Open File in the File menu in the main Netscape window.*

Figure 8.44 *The bookmarks file, complete with links to your saved sites, appears as a regular Web page.*

Opening a bookmarks file as a Web page

An easy way to see a bookmarks file without changing your regular bookmarks file is to open it as a Web page. Since the bookmarks file is in HTML format, like any other Web page, Netscape knows how to interpret it correctly, displaying folders in a large font, and making your bookmarks into links—automatically.

To open a bookmarks file as a Web page:

1. Save your bookmarks file, making sure to choose HTML Files in the List Files of Type pop-up menu. For more information, consult *Saving a bookmarks file* on page 87.

2. Choose Open File in the File menu in the main Netscape window **(Figure 8.43)**.

3. Choose the desired file and click Open. The bookmarks file is loaded into Netscape just like any other Web page **(Figure 8.44)**.

✔ Tip

■ You can also designate a bookmarks file as the page that Netscape displays automatically every time you launch the program, giving you immediate access to frequently visited sites. For more information, consult *Choosing a home page* on page 17.

Opening a bookmarks file as a Web page

Importing bookmarks

If you wish, you may *add* the bookmarks in a bookmarks file to your current bookmarks file, instead of replacing the existing bookmarks.

To import bookmarks:

1. Open the Bookmarks windows by choosing Bookmarks in the Window menu. The Bookmarks window appears.

2. Choose Import in the File menu in the Bookmarks window **(Figure 8.45)**. The Import dialog box appears.

3. Choose the bookmarks file that you wish to import **(Fig. 8.46)** and click Open. The bookmarks in the imported file are added to the current Bookmarks window **(Figure 8.47)**.

Figure 8.45 *To add bookmarks from another bookmark file to your current bookmark file, choose Import in the Bookmark window's File menu.*

Figure 8.46 *In the Import dialog box that appears, choose the bookmarks file that you wish to import.*

Figure 8.47 *The new bookmarks are added below the main folder in the current bookmarks file.*

The Mail Window

Figure 9.1 *By default, the Mail window has two top panes and one large bottom area.*

Figure 9.2 *The vertical stacking option displays the folders and messages at the left and the contents area to the right.*

Figure 9.3 *The stacking option divides the Mail window into three horizontal strips.*

The Mail window is Netscape's central filing area for all incoming and outgoing correspondence. From the Mail window, you can get, read, and send new mail, respond to mail, delete mail, and file mail.

Not all mail is equal. The Mail window lets you flag important letters and marks all mail as read or unread, letting you choose to list all mail or only that correspondence which you have not yet read.

The Mail window's filing system is fairly advanced, allowing you to create new folders for organizing incoming and outgoing correspondence, and to throw away those letters you no longer need.

Before you use the Mail or News windows, fill out the Server *(see page 260)* and Identity information *(see page 261).*

The parts of the Mail window

The Mail window is divided into three areas, or panes **(Figure 9.1)**. The top left pane contains the folders in which your mail is organized. When you click one of the mail folders, a list of the messages contained in the folder appears in the top right pane of the Mail window. Once you click in one of the e-mail messages, the contents of the letter appear in the bottom pane.

You can display the three panes of the Mail (or News) window in one of three ways: horizontally, which is the default **(Figure 9.1)**, vertically **(Figure 9.2)**, or stacked **(Figure 9.3)**. For more details, see page 258.

The parts of the Mail window

Opening the Mail window

The Mail window, together with the Browser and News windows, forms one leg of the Netscape triumvirate. You can have each type of window open at once, but to work with mail, the Mail window must be open and active.

To open the Mail window:

1. Choose Netscape Mail in the Window menu **(Figure 9.4)**. Netscape automatically checks your mail.

2. If the password dialog box appears, enter your password and click OK **(Figure 9.5)**. The Mail window appears **(Figure 9.6)**.

✔ Tip

■ You can also click the letter icon in the bottom right corner of all Netscape's windows to open the Mail window.

Saving your mail password

You can save your mail password so that Netscape doesn't ask for it each time you open the Mail window.

To save your Mail password:

1. Choose Mail and News Preferences in the Options menu **(Figure 9.7)**.

2. Click the Organization tab. The Organization preferences appear.

3. Click Remember Mail Password in the General section **(Figure 9.8)**.

4. Click OK.

Figure 9.4 *To open the Mail window, choose Netscape Mail in the Window menu.*

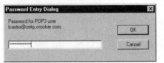

Figure 9.5 *If the Password Entry Dialog box appears, enter your password and click OK.*

Figure 9.6 *The Mail window has three panes. The top left pane shows the folders, the top right pane shows the letters in each folder and the bottom pane shows the contents of each letter.*

Figure 9.7 *Choose Mail and News Preferences in the Options menu.*

Figure 9.8 *Click the Organization tab and then click Remember Mail Password.*

Opening the Mail window

Netscape places new incoming mail in the Inbox.

The Outbox stores messages until they are sent.

The Trash holds deleted messages.

The Sent folder contains messages once they are sent.

Figure 9.9 *The Mail window contains four folders by default. You may add others as desired.*

The Mail window's four default folders

Netscape creates four default folders for filing mail: the Inbox, the Outbox, the Sent, and the Trash folders **(Figure 9.9)**.

Netscape stores the new, incoming mail in the Inbox. Once you've read them, you can move them to a more specific folder *(see page 99)*. Or if you're lazy like me, you can just leave them there.

The Outbox holds mail that you've written but haven't yet sent. For example, you can write several messages without being connected to your Internet server and then send them all at once *(see page 118)*. If you change your mind about sending a message, simply move it from the Outbox folder.

Once you've actually sent a message, Netscape transfers it to the Sent folder. You can choose to file sent messages in another folder, or just leave them there.

Finally, the Trash folder holds mail that you've deleted. For more information on deleting files, consult *Deleting messages and folders* on page 100. You can retrieve messages from the Trash (it doesn't even smell bad) until you decide to empty it. Once you've emptied the trash *(see page 101)*, the messages are truly gone.

Creating new folders

In addition to Netscape's default folders *(see page 93)*, you can create as many of your own as your hard disk space will allow. Folders are helpful for organizing your mail once you've received or sent it.

To create a new folder:

1. In the Mail window's File menu, choose New Folder **(Figure 9.10)**.

2. Enter a name for the folder in the dialog box that appears and click OK **(Figure 9.11)**. The new folder appears in the left pane of the Mail window **(Figure 9.12)**.

✔ Tips

■ Netscape won't let you create folders inside other folders directly, but it can be done. For more information, consult *Nesting folders* on page 95.

■ It's a little tricky to change a folder's name once it's created. The easiest way is to create a new folder with the correct name and drag any messages it contains to the new folder. The hard way is by finding the desired mail folder file (usually in the Mail folder inside the Netscape folder on your hard disk) and changing the name of both it and the corresponding .snm file.

■ The Add Folder command is not for adding new folders, but rather for importing the contents of one folder into another. For more information, consult *Importing messages from another folder* on page 96.

Figure 9.10 *Choose New Folder in the Mail window's File menu.*

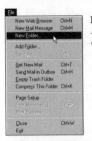

Figure 9.11 *In the dialog box, type the name for the new folder and click OK.*

Figure 9.12 *The new folder appears in the upper left pane of the Mail window.*

Figure 9.13 *The original folder.*

Figure 9.14 *Hierarchical folders in the Mail window.*

Nesting folders

There is no menu command for creating folders inside an existing folder. However, if you know how to create folders on your PC, you can create nested folders in the Mail window.

To create nested folders:

1. Close the Mail window.

2. Switch to the Explorer.

3. Open the Mail folder, which is inside the Netscape folder.

4. Choose New Folder in the Explorer's File menu to create new folders as desired inside the Mail folder.

5. Organize the existing folders (which appear as files—one with and one without the .snm extension) in the new folders.

6. Return to Netscape and open the Mail window. Voilà! Hierarchical, nested folders **(Figure 9.14)**.

✔ Tips

■ You can't create new, hierarchical folders inside folders created by Netscape. Instead, create your own folders in the Explorer, and then transfer messages to them as described on page 99.

■ Don't worry about the .snm files. These are indexes that Netscape will automatically generate as necessary.

Nesting folders

Importing messages from another folder

Netscape stores all the messages in each folder in a single file. You can copy these mail folder files between computers and then open them to access the messages they contain. You can also open the mail folder files in your own Mail window to copy the messages into a new folder, but I'm not quite sure why you'd want to.

To import messages from another folder:

1. Choose Add Folder in the Mail window's File menu **(Figure 9.15)**. The Open dialog box appears.

2. Find and select the mail folder file that you wish to import and click Open **(Figure 9.16)**. The folder file is imported into the left pane of the Mail window **(Figure 9.17)**.

3. Click the folder file to see the messages it contains.

✔ Tips

■ Generally, mail folder files are stored in the Mail folder inside the Netscape folder. You will probably have to choose All Files in the Files of Type submenu to see them. Don't use the files that end in .snm (which are simply indexes of the file folders), but rather the ones with no extension.

■ The name of the new folder in the Mail window is the path to the selected mail folder file. To change the folder name, see the tip on page 94.

Figure 9.15 *Choose Add Folder in the Mail window's File menu.*

Figure 9.16 *Choose a mail folder file in the Open dialog box and click Open.*

Figure 9.17 *The new mail folder appears in the left pane of the Mail window.*

Figure 9.18 *Hold down Shift and click to select several messages in a row.*

Figure 9.19 *Hold down Ctrl and click to select several messages that are not one after the other.*

Figure 9.20 *Select a folder and then choose Select Flagged Messages in the Edit menu to select all the flagged messages in the folder.*

Figure 9.21 *All of the flagged messages are selected.*

Selecting messages

There are several ways to select messages that make it easier to file, read, or delete a particular group of messages.

To select more than one message:

Hold down Shift and click to add one or more messages that are next to the currently selected message **(Figure 9.18)**. Hold down Ctrl and click to add one or more messages that are not next to the currently selected one **(Figure 9.19)**.

You can also select all the flagged messages in a folder, perhaps prior to moving them to another folder en masse. For more information about flags, consult *Flagging messages* on page 103.

To select the flagged messages:

1. Select the desired folder.

2. Choose Select Flagged Messages in the Edit menu **(Figure 9.20)**. All of the flagged messages in the currently selected folder are selected **(Figure 9.21)**.

Selecting messages

You can also select all the messages in a thread (in a folder) in order to move, copy, or delete them at once. For more information about threads, consult *Threading messages* on page 105.

To select a thread:

1. Select one of the messages in the thread.

2. Choose Select Thread in the Edit menu **(Figure 9.22)**. Each message that belongs to the thread is selected **(Figure 9.23)**.

Last but not least, you can select all the messages in a folder.

To select all the messages in a folder:

1. Select the desired folder.

2. Choose Select All Messages (Ctrl+A) in the Edit menu **(Figure 9.24)**. All the messages in the chosen folder are selected **(Figure 9.25)**.

✔ Tips

■ You can't select messages in more than one folder at a time.

■ Once you've selected a group of messages, you can move or copy them to another folder, or delete them. For more information on moving and copying messages, consult *Moving and copying messages* on page 99. For more information on deleting messages, consult *Deleting messages and folders* on page 100.

Figure 9.22 *Select a message and then choose Select Thread in the Edit menu to select all the related messages.*

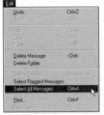

Figure 9.23 *All the messages related to the original message, that is, in the message's thread, are selected.*

Figure 9.24 *Select a folder and then choose Select All Messages in the Edit menu to select every message in the folder.*

Figure 9.25 *All the messages in the folder are selected.*

Figure 9.26 *Select the desired message.*

Figure 9.27 *Choose the destination folder in the Move submenu in the Message menu.*

Figure 9.28 *The message is removed from its earlier location (the Inbox now has only 30 messages) and placed in the desired folder.*

Figure 9.29 *Choose the desired folder in the Copy submenu in the Message menu.*

Figure 9.30 *The message remains in the previous location (the Inbox still has 30 messages), and is copied to the selected folder (which now has 2).*

Moving and copying messages

Generally, in order to keep things organized, you move messages from Netscape's default folders (e.g., the Inbox and Sent folders) to the folders you have created. *Copying* moves the message to the new folder and leaves a copy in the old one.

To move messages to a different folder:

1. Select the message(s) **(Figure 9.26)**.

2. Choose the desired destination folder under Move in the Message menu, **(Fig. 9.27)**. The message disappears from the current folder and is transferred to the selected one **(Fig. 9.28)**.

To copy messages to a different folder:

1. Select the message(s) **(Figure 9.26)**.

2. Choose the desired destination folder under Copy in the Message menu **(Figure 9.29)**. The message remains in the current folder and is also copied to the selected one **(Fig. 9.30)**.

✔ Tips

■ You can also drag messages from one folder to another. Hold down Ctrl while you drag to copy.

■ Use the special selecting commands *(see page 97)* to select more than one message before moving or copying.

■ You cannot move or copy messages to the Outbox folder. The only way to place messages there is by sending them with Deferred Delivery selected. For details, consult *Composing messages offline* on page 118.

Deleting messages and folders

Once you no longer need a message, you can delete it in order to conserve space on your hard disk and keep your Mail window reasonably neat.

To delete a message:

1. Select the desired message(s) **(Figure 9.31)**.

2. Choose Delete Message from the Edit menu or press Delete—not Backspace **(Figure 9.32)**. No alert box will appear to confirm the deletion. The message simply disappears from the current folder and is moved to the Trash folder **(Figure 9.33)**.

You can only delete a folder after you've deleted all the messages it contains.

To delete a folder:

1. Select the desired folder.

2. Choose Delete Folder in the Edit menu or press Delete—not Backspace **(Figure 9.34)**. No alert box will appear to confirm the deletion. The folder simply disappears forever.

✔ Tips

■ To recover a message you've deleted, simply drag it out of the Trash folder.

■ You can also drag a message to the Trash folder to delete it.

■ Press Ctrl+Z immediately after deleting one or more messages or a folder to restore the items to their previous location.

Figure 9.31 *Choose the message you wish to delete.*

Figure 9.32 *Choose Delete Message in the Edit menu (or press the Delete key).*

Figure 9.33 *The message disappears from the current folder and is placed in the Trash.*

Figure 9.34 *To delete a folder, select it and then choose Delete Folder in the Edit menu.*

Deleting messages and folders

Figure 9.35 *To permanently remove the deleted messages, choose Empty Trash Folder in the File menu.*

Figure 9.36 *The Trash folder is empty.*

Figure 9.37 *Select a folder. The amount of data wasted is shown in the status area at the bottom of the window.*

Figure 9.38 *Choose Compress This Folder in the File menu.*

Figure 9.39 *The status area indicates that the compressed folder no longer wastes disk space.*

Conserving disk space

When you delete a message, it is not permanently deleted, but instead is placed in the Trash folder. You can retrieve an item from the Trash folder at any time before emptying it *(see page 99)*. Empty the trash to permanently remove the messages it contains.

To empty the Trash folder:

Choose Empty Trash Folder in the File menu **(Fig. 9.35)**. No alert box appears, nor will the Undo command make your messages come back. The Trash folder simply appears empty **(Figure 9.36)**.

Another way to reduce the amount of space taken up by your folders and messages is by compressing your folders.

To compress a folder:

1. Select the folder you wish to compress **(Figure 9.37)**.

2. Choose Compress This Folder in the File menu **(Figure 9.38)**. The folder is compressed **(Figure 9.39)**.

✔ Tips

■ The amount of space you can recover by compressing a folder is shown in the status area of the Mail window when the folder is selected.

■ Emptying the trash compresses all the folders automatically.

■ Compressing a folder does not affect any of the messages it contains. It simply recovers wasted space that is generated when you move messages from one folder to another.

Putting your messages in order

You can view your messages in order of Date, Subject, Sender (or Recipient, if you're in the Outbox or Sent folders), or even by Message Number. They may be sorted in ascending or descending order, although the latter is the default option. Mail folders (and newsgroups) are always displayed in alphabetical order.

To put your messages in order:

1. Select By Date, By Subject, By Sender, or By Message Number under Sort in the Mail window's View menu **(Figure 9.40)**. The messages are sorted according to the criteria chosen.

2. Toggle the Ascending option under Sort in the View menu to list the letters in ascending (when the option is checked) or descending order **(Figure 9.41)**.

✔ Tips

■ The Recipient header appears only when you are viewing the Sent or Outbox folders (since the Sender will almost always be the same: you). To sort messages by Recipient, choose By Sender in the Sort menu.

■ You can also click the column heading (Sender/Recipient, Subject, or Date) to sort your messages by the contents of that column **(Figure 9.42, Figure 9.43, and Figure 9.44)**. To sort by Message number, you have to use the menu.

Figure 9.40
Choose By Sender under Sort in the View menu to put the messages in order by sender.

Figure 9.41
Choose Ascending under Sort in the View menu to choose the direction in which to sort.

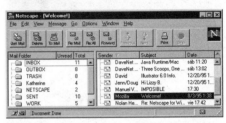

Figure 9.42 *Descending order, by sender.*

Figure 9.43 *Descending order, by Subject. Notice that "Re:" is ignored.*

Figure 9.44 *Descending order, by date.*

Putting your messages in order

Figure 9.45 *Select the message you wish to flag.*

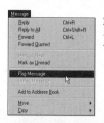

Figure 9.46 *Choose Flag Message in the Message menu.*

Figure 9.47 *A little red flag appears next to the message.*

Flagging messages

In a busy mailbox, it's sometimes hard to keep your eye on an important piece of mail. One easy way to make a message stand out is to mark or flag it.

To flag or unflag a message:

1. Select the desired message in the right pane of the Mail window **(Figure 9.45)**.

2. Choose Flag Message in the Message window **(Figure 9.46)**. A checkmark next to the command indicates that the message is flagged. Choose the command again to toggle it. A little red flag appears in the Flagged column next to the flagged message **(Figure 9.47)**. The flag disappears when you unflag the message.

✔ Tips

■ You can flag a message (or remove its flag) by clicking in the Flagged column ◪ next to the desired message.

■ You can navigate through only the flagged messages using the First Flagged, Next Flagged, and Previous Flagged commands in the Go menu. For more information on getting from message to message, consult *Navigating through your messages* on page 114.

Flagging messages

Marking mail as read or unread

When you receive new mail, Netscape marks it with a green diamond so that you know that it's new. Once you've read a message, the mark disappears. You can choose to restore the Unread mark to remind yourself to return to that message at a later date. You can also mark mail as read, even if you haven't read it—perhaps because you can tell from the Subject line that the message is not of interest to you.

To mark mail as read or unread:

1. Select the desired messages in the Mail window's right pane **(Fig. 9.48)**.

2. In the Message menu, choose Mark as Unread or Mark as Read **(Fig. 9.49)**. A green diamond appears next to messages that are unread and disappears for messages that you've read or marked as read **(Figure 9.50)**.

✔ Tips

■ You can also mark a message as read or unread by clicking in the Read column (the one with the green diamond) next to the desired message.

■ You can navigate through the unread messages using the First Unread, Next Unread, and Previous Unread commands in the Go menu. For more information about moving from message to message, consult *Navigating through your messages* on page 114.

■ You can mark a single message as read without opening it (which automatically marks it as read). The trick is to click right on the diamond, not on the title of the message.

Figure 9.48 *Choose the unread messages that you wish to mark as read.*

Figure 9.49 *Choose Mark as Read in the Message menu.*

Figure 9.50 *The newly "read" messages appear in plain text and the green diamonds disappear.*

Marking mail as read or unread

Figure 9.51 *Unthreaded messages appear independently in the Mail window's right pane.*

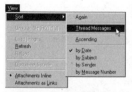

Figure 9.52 *Choose Thread Messages under Sort in the View menu to relate messages with similar subjects.*

Figure 9.53 *Threaded messages appear in hierarchical form with the original message at the top and replies below and to the right.*

Figure 9.54 *Click the minus sign to the left of the original message's letter icon to hide the replies. Click it again (it will have turned into a plus sign as shown above) to show the replies.*

Threading messages

Netscape can relate all the replies (and replies to replies) that are generated from a single original message into a wonderful invention called a *thread*. This makes it easy to follow a particular conversation from start to finish even if you have a busy mailbox. You can choose to view your e-mail in threads, or as individual messages.

To thread messages:

1. Choose Thread Messages under Sort in the Mail window's View menu **(Figure 9.52)**. The option will have a check next to it when it is active. Choose the option again to toggle it. Each message that is related to another will appear underneath the parent message, connected by a dotted, hierarchical line **(Figure 9.53)**.

2. Click the minus sign next to a threaded message group to hide the replies beneath it. Click a plus sign next to a threaded message group to reveal the replies beneath it **(Figure 9.54)**.

Threading messages

Changing the size of the panes

You can change the size of each of a window's three panes, according to the task at hand. For example, if you're filing mail, you'll want the two upper panes as large as possible **(Figure 9.57)**. On the other hand, if you're reading a series of messages, it will be better to make the lower pane as large as possible **(Figure 9.58)**.

To change the size of the panes:

1. Place the pointer over one of the separators between the panes. The cursor changes into a double-headed arrow **(Figure 9.55)**.

2. Click with the mouse and drag to make the panes larger or smaller **(Figure 9.56, Figure 9.57, and Figure 9.58)**.

✔ Tips

■ You can resize the entire window by dragging in the usual way.

■ If you make the panes so short that not all the contents can be seen, scroll bars will appear to give you access. This does not happen if you make a pane too narrow; in that case, the hidden material stays out of sight.

■ If you make the window too short to see the bottom pane, you won't be able to see the contents of your messages, and scrolling won't help.

■ When you change the width of the panes, either by moving the pane separator as described above or by changing the window size, the width of the *columns* is not affected. For more information, consult *Changing the columns* on page 107.

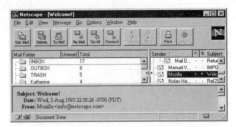

Figure 9.55 *To reduce the amount of wasted space in the left pane, place the pointer on the pane's border, click and drag to resize.*

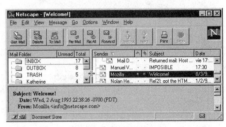

Figure 9.56 *Now there is more room in the right pane to display more information.*

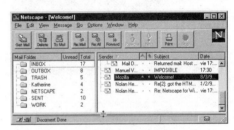

Figure 9.57 *Drag the middle border to the bottom to hide the contents of messages (and have more room for folder and message titles).*

Figure 9.58 *Drag the middle border to the top to hide the folders and message titles and thus have more space for the message itself.*

Changing the size of the panes

Figure 9.59 *Some of the Senders' names are cut off. To make the Sender column wider, click the right border of the column and drag to resize.*

Figure 9.60 *Once the column is wider, the Senders' complete names can be seen.*

Figure 9.61 *To move the Subject column next to the Sender column, simply click the Subject header and drag to the right of the Sender header.*

Changing the columns

There is a lot of information jammed into eight columns between two panes in the Mail (and News) window. You can adjust the width or order of the columns to suit your particular task.

To change the column width:

1. Place the cursor on the left border of the column's title **(Figure 9.59)**.

2. Drag to adjust the size of the column **(Figure 9.60)**.

You may find it easier to organize your messages if the columns are arranged in a special order. For example, you could put the Marked and Read columns to the left of the Sender (or Recipient) column.

To change the column order:

Click in the desired column's title and drag it to the new position **(Figure 9.61)**. The other columns are adjusted accordingly.

✔ Tip

■ If you aren't interested in a particular column's data, drag it to the right-most position in the pane. Then, either make the other columns larger or the pane or window smaller so that the undesired columns are hidden from view.

Changing the columns

Changing your messages' appearance

You can change the appearance of messages in the Mail (and News) window to make them easier to read.

To change your messages' appearance:

1. Choose Mail and News Preferences in the Options menu **(Figure 9.62)**. The Mail and News Preferences window appears.

2. Click the Appearance tab at the top left corner of the window to show the Appearance preferences **(Fig. 9.63)**.

3. In the first section, choose Fixed Width Font to show your messages in a font like Courier or Variable Width Font to show your messages in a font like Times or Helvetica.

4. In the second section, choose a style and a size for the quoted text in your messages.

5. Click OK to close the Preferences window. The messages in the Mail (and News) window will now appear with the type of font selected. Quotes will appear with the style selected **(Figure 9.64)**.

✔ Tips

■ You can specify the actual fonts in the Fonts tab of the General Preferences dialog box *(see page 247)*.

■ Unfortunately, these options have no effect on the Message Composition window (where they would be particularly handy).

Figure 9.62 *Choose Mail and News Preferences in the Options menu.*

Figure 9.63 *Click the Appearance tab at the top left corner of the window to show the Appearances preferences. Then choose the desired font type and style.*

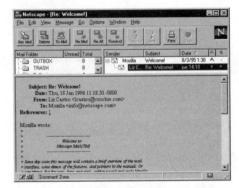

Figure 9.64 *Notice how the entire note is displayed in a Variable Width Font (Times in this case) and that the quoted part of the note is in italics.*

Figure 9.65 *Choose Wrap Long Lines in the Mail window's View menu.*

Wrapping long lines

Not all e-mail programs include returns in their messages. For example, earlier versions of Netscape inserted returns in outgoing messages according to the width of Message Composition window when the message was created. If you receive a message whose lines are too long to read comfortably on screen, you can choose to add additional returns to make it easier to read.

To wrap long lines to view messages better:

Choose Wrap Long Lines in the Mail Window's View menu **(Figure 9.65)**. Additional returns will be added to the viewed messages in order to view them in entirety on screen.

✔ Tip

■ The Wrap Long Lines option in the Mail window's View menu is *not* the same as the Wrap Long Lines option in the Message Composition window's View menu. The former controls only the appearance of incoming messages while the latter actually adds returns to outgoing messages.

Unscrambling ROT-13 messages

Many e-mail programs (although not Netscape) allow their users to lightly encrypt messages in order to shield them from prying eyes. However, since the encryption (ROT-13) is easily undone at the other side, this type of protection is most commonly applied to messages with content that may be offensive, thereby giving access only to those who wish to have it.

To unscramble messages encrypted with ROT-13:

1. View the message as usual **(Figure 9.66)**.

2. Choose Unscramble (ROT-13) in the Mail window's View menu **(Figure 9.67)**. The message appears unscrambled **(Figure 9.68)**.

✔ Tip

■ Although Netscape has no command for creating ROT-13 messages, you can create them by sending a message to yourself, viewing it unscrambled (which if it wasn't scrambled now makes it scrambled) and then copying the scrambled text to a new Message Composition window.

■ ROT-13 is an extremely simple code. It simply replaces each letter with the letter that comes 13 letters later in the alphabet (*n* for *a*, for example). Don't use it for sensitive material.

Figure 9.66 *The original message appears unreadable in the Mail window.*

Figure 9.67 *Choose Unscramble (ROT-13) in the Mail window's View menu.*

Figure 9.68 *Once unscrambled, the message is much easier to read.*

Reading and Sending Mail

Figure 10.1 *Click the letter icon in the lower right corner of the Netscape window to retrieve your mail from the server.*

Figure 10.2 *Another way to check your mail is by choosing Get New Mail in the Mail window's File menu.*

Figure 10.3 *Last but not least, you can also click the Get Mail button at the left of the toolbar to check your mail.*

Figure 10.4 *Regardless of the method you use, Netscape places new mail in the Inbox, and shows both the Inbox and the message title in bold.*

You can use Netscape to compose and send new mail, or to read or reply to mail that you've received from others.

Getting new mail

Once you have a new e-mail address, checking to see if someone has actually sent you something becomes almost an obsession. Luckily, Netscape gives you several ways to check your electronic mailbox.

To get new mail from the browser or News window:

Click the letter icon in the bottom right corner of the screen **(Figure 10.1)**. Netscape will open the Mail window, ask for your password if necessary *(see page 92)*, consult your server, and finally show you your new mail (if you have any).

If you've already opened the Mail window, you can click the letter icon or choose the command from the menu.

To get new mail from the Mail window:

Choose Get New Mail in the Mail window's File menu **(Figure 10.2)**. The new mail, if any, will be displayed in the Inbox folder **(Figure 10.4)**.

✔ Tip

■ You can also click the Get Mail button on the Mail window's toolbar to get mail **(Figure 10.3)**.

Having Netscape check for mail periodically

When you are connected to the Internet, you can have Netscape check for mail every few minutes all on its own and alert you when you've received something. Obviously, if you're not connected, Netscape won't be able to tell if you have mail.

To have Netscape check for mail periodically:

1. Choose Mail and News Preferences in the Options menu **(Figure 10.5)**. The Preferences dialog box appears.

2. Click the Servers tab at the top of the dialog box.

3. At the bottom of the Mail section, click Every and then press the Tab key **(Figure 10.6)**.

4. Enter a number next to the Every text box to determine how often Netscape will check the server for mail.

5. Click OK to close the Preferences dialog box.

✔ Tips

■ Netscape doesn't automatically *copy* mail from the server—it just checks to see if there is any. If there is, it notifies you with an exclamation point next to the letter icon **(Figure 10.7)**. You still have to *get* your mail *(see page 111)*.

■ If you don't want Netscape constantly checking for mail, choose Never in step 3.

■ Netscape will only check for mail automatically if you have saved your mail password *(see page 92)*.

Figure 10.5 *Choose Mail and News Preferences from the Options menu.*

Figure 10.6 *First click Servers at the top of the box. Then select Every next to Check for Mail and type a number in the minutes box.*

Figure 10.7 *A plain letter icon means you have no letters waiting on the server. A question mark means Netscape can't tell if you have any mail waiting (you're probably not connected). An exclamation point means you have mail waiting on the server.*

Figure 10.8 *New mail is placed in the Inbox, and both the Inbox and the message titles themselves are shown in bold face. Click a message title in the right pane to open it.*

Figure 10.9 *The new message is displayed in the lower pane of the Mail window. (I've also made the entire Mail window longer here, to be able to see all three panes.)*

Figure 10.10 *To hide all but the unread messages in the upper right pane of the Mail window, choose Show Only Unread Messages in the Options menu.*

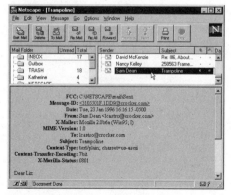

Figure 10.11 *Choose All under Show Headers to view additional information about a message. Choose Brief to show just the Re and To fields.*

Reading mail

Once you have received new mail, you can open it and read it. You can also re-read mail received earlier, or read mail that you have sent to others.

To read mail:

1. Click the folder in the top left pane that contains the e-mail you want to read **(Figure 10.8)**. You'll find new mail in the Inbox folder. The contents of the folder appear in the top right pane.

2. Click the message that you want to read **(Figure 10.9)**. The contents of the message appear in the bottom pane of the window.

3. Use the scroll bars in the lower pane to move around in the note.

✔ Tips

■ You can have the Mail window display only those messages that you haven't read yet by choosing Show Only Unread Messages in the Options menu **(Figure 10.10)**.

■ You can show additional information about a message **(Figure 10.11)**, including the route it took to get to you (which is sometimes useful for exposing fraudulent messages), by choosing All under Show Headers in the Options menu. Choose Brief to show just the Re and To fields.

■ Thankfully, the Mail window can be rearranged according to the task at hand. When reading, make the bottom pane as large as possible. When filing, make the upper panes larger. For more information on changing the panes, consult *Changing the size of the panes* on page 106.

Reading mail

Navigating through your messages

Netscape's Go menu makes it easy to move from one message to the next.

To open the next message:

Choose Next Message in the Go menu or press the down arrow **(Figure 10.12)**.

To open the previous message:

Choose Previous Message in the Go menu or press the up arrow.

✔ Tips

■ The up and down arrows only work if the cursor is in the upper-right pane of the window. If you've clicked in the lower pane, the up and down arrows simply navigate you through that particular message.

■ You can jump to the first unread message by choosing First Unread in the Go menu. Jump to the next and previous unread messages by choosing Next Unread and Previous Unread, respectively **(Fig. 10.13)**. (*Next* in this case means *below* the current message. *Previous* means *above* the current message, and does not refer to the unread message you read before the current one.) For more information, consult *Marking mail as read or unread* on page 104.

■ Jump to the first flagged message by choosing First Flagged in the Go menu **(Fig. 10.14)**. Jump to the next and previous flagged messages by choosing Next Flagged and Previous Flagged. For more information, consult *Flagging messages* on page 103.

Figure 10.12 *Click Next Message or Previous Message in the Go menu to move from one message to another.*

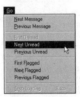

Figure 10.13 *Choose any of the Unread commands (First Unread, Next Unread, or Previous Unread) to navigate only among those messages that you have not yet read.*

Figure 10.14 *Choose First, Next, or Previous Flagged to navigate among the marked messages.*

Figure 10.15 *Choose New Mail Message in the File menu to start a new e-mail message.*

Figure 10.16 *You can also click the To: Mail button on the toolbar to start a new message.*

Figure 10.17 *In the Message Composition window, type the recipient's address in the Mail To field, type a Subject, add an Attachment, if desired, and type the contents of the message.*

Figure 10.18 *Once your satisfied with the message, choose Send Now in the File menu. (For deferred delivery, consult Composing messages offline on page 118.)*

Figure 10.19 *You can also send a finished message by clicking the Send button at the top left of the Message Composition window.*

Composing a new message

Somehow, e-mail is a thousand times easier to write than a conventional letter.

To compose a new message:

1. Choose New Mail Message in the File menu **(Figure 10.15)** or click the To: Mail button **(Fig. 10.16)**. A fresh Message Composition window appears.

2. Type the recipient's address in the Mail To field. Separate multiple addresses with a comma **(Fig. 10.17)**.

3. Type the address(es) where you wish to send "carbon" copies in the Cc box.

4. Type a subject for the message. As the most visible part of the message, it is often used as the criteria for filing.

5. Click the Attachment button to attach a file or URL *(see page 126)*.

6. Type the contents of the message in the area at the bottom of the window.

7. Choose Send in the File menu or click the Send button to send the message **(Figure 10.18 and Figure 10.19)**.

✔ Tips

■ Click the Address button (or any of the Mail To, Cc, etc. buttons) to make the Address book appear.

■ For information on deferred sending, consult *Composing messages offline* on page 118.

■ Double click a name in the Address book to open a new message automatically addressed to that person.

■ If you don't use the Wrap Long Lines command, make sure the Message Composition window is not too wide.

Composing a new message

Viewing or hiding the parts of a message

A message can have up to nine sections: From, Reply To, Mail To, Mail Cc, Mail Bcc, Newsgroups, Followups To, Subject, and Attachment. You can show or hide any combination of these message parts.

To view or hide parts of a message:

1. Choose New Mail Message in the File menu to open the Message Composition window **(Figure 10.20)**. By default, you'll see the Subject, Mail To, Cc, and Attachment fields.

2. Choose the desired message part from the View menu **(Figure 10.22)**. When the option has a checkmark, that message part will be visible **(Figure 10.23)**. You can also choose Show All in the View menu to view all nine message parts.

✔ Tips

■ Some of the message parts are self explanatory. Others are not so clear. *From* is your e-mail address. *Reply To* is the address where replies should be sent. *Mail Cc* is for sending a "carbon" copy of the message to others. *Mail Bcc* is for sending a copy to others without the recipient knowing. *Newsgroups* shows the newsgroup to which you wish to post the message *(see page 156).*

■ In Netscape 3, the Message Composition's View menu has a new option: Wrap Long Lines, which when activated, ensures that outgoing messages have the proper line breaks. You should generally leave it active.

Figure 10.20 *Choose New Mail Message in the File menu to open the Message Composition window.*

Figure 10.21 *By default, the Message Composition window shows the Mail To, Cc, Subject, and Attachment fields as well as the contents.*

Figure 10.22 *Choose the message part that you wish to see in the View menu. Visible parts are shown with a checkmark. (Choose a checked item to uncheck it and hide it in the Message Composition window.)*

Figure 10.23 *After choosing Reply To in the View menu, the corresponding field is displayed in the Message Composition window.*

Viewing or hiding the parts of a message

Figure 10.24 *Select the message to which you wish to reply.*

Figure 10.25 *Choose Reply in the Mail window's Message menu.*

Figure 10.26 *You can also click the Re: Mail button in the middle of the toolbar.*

Figure 10.27 *The Mail To and Subject fields are automatically filled in and the contents may contain a quoted version of the original message.*

Figure 10.28 *Type the new material and Send.*

Replying to a message you've received

Replying to someone else's message instead of creating a new message *(see page 115)* has certain advantages: the addressing is done automatically and you can choose to quote the original letter in your reply.

To reply to a message you've received:

1. Select the message to which you wish to reply **(Figure 10.24)**.

2. Choose Reply in the Message window **(Figure 10.25)** or click the Re: Mail button on the toolbar **(Figure 10.26)**. The Message Composition window appears. The Mail To box is automatically filled in. The original letter may or may not be quoted in the message area *(see page 121)*. The subject area contains the original subject preceded by "Re:" **(Figure 10.27)**.

3. Type the body of the message **(Figure 10.28)**.

4. Click the Send button or choose the Send command in the File menu *(see page 115)*. Unless you have chosen Deferred Delivery in the Options menu *(see page 118)*, your reply is sent immediately.

✔ Tip

■ If the original message was addressed to more than one person, you can reply to all of them at once by selecting Reply to All in the Message menu, or by clicking Re: All on the toolbar.

Composing messages offline

If you have a dial-up Internet connection, you can compose messages offline and then send them all together once you've connected. Not only does this save a lot of money, but it'll let you relax as you write.

To compose messages offline:

1. Disconnect from the Internet without quitting Netscape (or launch Netscape without connecting to the Internet).

2. Choose New Mail Message in the File menu or select a message and choose Reply in the Message menu **(Figure 10.29)**. The Message Composition window appears.

3. In the Message Composition window's Options menu, choose Deferred Delivery **(Figure 10.30)**.

4. Compose the message as usual *(see page 115)*.

5. Choose Send Later in the File menu or click the Send button in the Message Composition window **(Figure 10.31 and Figure 10.32)**. The message is stored in the Outbox.

6. When you're ready to send the message(s) consult *Sending the messages in the Outbox* on page 119.

✔ Tips

■ To return to immediate sending, open the Message Composition window and choose Immediate delivery in the Options menu.

■ If you change your mind about sending a message in the Outbox, simply drag it to another folder *(see page 99)* or delete it *(see page 100)*.

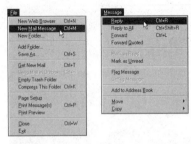

Figure 10.29 *Either choose New Mail Message in the File menu, or select a message and choose Reply or Reply to All in the Message menu.*

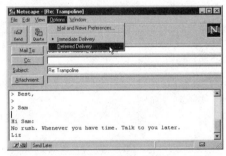

Figure 10.30 *Choose Deferred Delivery in the Message Composition's Options menu to hold off sending your messages until later (presumably when you've connected up again).*

Figure 10.31 *When you've finished composing your message, choose Send Later in the File menu.*

Figure 10.32 *You can also click the Send button on the toolbar. Although its title doesn't change, the Send (Later) button does acquire a little clock to indicate that you've chosen Deferred Delivery.*

Composing messages offline

Figure 10.33 *As you compose messages offline and "send" them as described on page 118, they are stored in the Outbox.*

Figure 10.34 *Once you've connected to the Internet and are ready to send your messages, choose Send Mail in Outbox in the File menu.*

Figure 10.35 *Once you send the messages in the Outbox, they are moved from the Outbox folder to the Sent folder.*

Sending the messages in the Outbox

If you've composed several messages offline—both e-mail and news *(see page 159)*—you can choose to send them when it is convenient for you.

To send the messages in the Outbox:

1. If desired, click the Outbox in the Mail window to see which messages you've stored for later delivery.

2. Open your Internet connection.

3. With the Mail window active, choose Send Mail in Outbox in the File menu **(Figure 10.34)**. All your stored mail and news postings are sent. Netscape automatically transfers sent messages to the Sent folder **(Figure 10.35)**. For more information on the Sent folder, consult *The Mail window's four default folders* on page 93.

4. Close your Internet connection, if desired.

✔ Tips

■ If the Send Mail in Outbox option does not appear, make sure the Mail window is open and active.

■ Both the Outbox and the Sent folders show the Recipient of a message instead of its Sender, since the Sender is usually you.

Sending the messages in the Outbox

Editing messages in the Outbox

Unfortunately, it's not as easy as it should be to edit a message once you've stored it in the Outbox for deferred delivery *(see page 118)*. However, you can leave Netscape and use any text editor or word processor to do the trick.

To edit a message in the Outbox:

1. Close the Mail window.

2. Open any text editor.

3. Choose Open in the text editor's File menu.

4. Select the Outbox file, which you'll find in the Mail folder, inside the Netscape folder, on your hard disk **(Figure 10.37)**.

5. Edit the document **(Figure 10.38)**.

6. Save the document. Be sure to save the file in Text Only format. Do not change its name.

7. Return to Netscape and open the Mail window. Click the Outbox folder and then click the message to review the changes **(Figure 10.39)**.

✔ Tip

■ If you change your mind about sending a message that you've stored in the Outbox for deferred delivery, you can move *(see page 99)* or delete the message *(see page 100)* so that it does not reach the recipient. Of course, you have to do this before actually sending the message.

Figure 10.36 *You can edit the messages that you have deferred for later sending (in the Outbox).*

Figure 10.37 *In the Open dialog box of your word processor, choose the Outbox file.*

Figure 10.38 *Change the message as desired. (You may have to scroll down to find it.)*

Figure 10.39 *Click on the message in the Outbox to confirm the changes.*

Figure 10.40 *Choose Mail and News Preferences in the Options menu.*

Figure 10.41 *Click the Composition tab and then check Automatically quote original message when replying at the bottom of the window.*

Quoting every message

When you reply to a message, you can have Netscape automatically "quote" the original correspondence, so that the recipient readily knows what you are responding to. Each line of a quoted message is preceded with a greater than sign (>), by Internet convention, and the original author's name is inserted at the beginning of the quote.

To quote every message:

1. Choose Mail and News Preferences in the Options menu **(Figure 10.40)**. The Preferences dialog box appears.

2. Click the Composition tab at the top of the window. The Composition preferences appear.

3. Mark the option Automatically quote original message when replying at the bottom of the dialog box **(Fig. 10.41)**. Leave the option unchecked if you don't want Netscape to include a copy of the original message every time you reply.

4. Click OK to close the Preferences dialog box. From now on, each message you reply to will automatically include a copy of the original message.

✔ Tip

- You can choose how the quoted material appears in the Mail window (although not in the Message Composition window). For more details, consult *Changing your messages' appearance* on page 108.

Quoting individual messages

Having Netscape quote every message you reply to can get a little tiresome, especially if the original messages are often long. You can turn off Netscape's automatic quoting and then quote messages individually, when desired.

To quote individual messages:

1. Generally, you will have turned Netscape's automatic feature off, as described on page 121, unchecking the option in step 3 **(Figure 10.42)**.

2. Reply to a message in the normal way **(Figure 10.43 and Figure 10.44)**. See page 117 for details. The Message Composition window appears.

3. In the Message Composition window click the Quote button or choose Include Original Text in the File menu **(Figure 10.45 and Figure 10.46)**. The original message appears in the message area, labeled with the original author's name. Each line of a quote is preceded by greater than signs (>), as is the convention on the Internet **(Figure 10.47)**.

4. You may cut out parts of the quote if you don't wish to quote the entire original message. Simply select them with the mouse and choose Cut from the Edit menu, or press Backspace.

✔ Tip

■ You can change the way a quote is displayed in the Mail window, but unfortunately, not in the Message Composition window. For more details, consult *Changing your messages' appearance* on page 108.

Figure 10.42 *Uncheck the Automatically quote original messages option in the Composition tab of the preferences dialog box (cf Figure 10.41).*

Figure 10.43 *Choose Reply or Reply to All in the Message menu.*

Figure 10.44 *Or click the Re: Mail or Re: All buttons on the toolbar.*

Figure 10.45 *The Mail To and Subject fields are automatically filled in. Click the Quote button to quote the original message.*

Figure 10.46 *Or choose Include Original Text in the Message Composition window's File menu.*

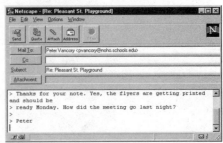

Figure 10.47 *The original message is quoted.*

Figure 10.48 *Select the material you wish to quote in the original document. (This is from Notepad.)*

Figure 10.49 *Choose Copy to copy the material to the clipboard.*

Figure 10.50 *Switch back to the Message Composition window, and choose Paste as Quotation in the Edit menu.*

Figure 10.51 *The copied material is pasted in the contents area with a greater than sign (>) at the beginning of each line (well, paragraph).*

Custom quoting

If you don't want to quote the entire message, or if you want to quote several parts of various messages, you can use Netscape's custom quoting feature to add greater than signs at the beginning of each line of text.

To quote a part of a message:

1. Select the text that you wish to quote **(Figure 10.48)**. The text may be from any file; it doesn't have to be from a message received with Netscape.

2. Choose Copy (Ctrl+C) in the Edit menu **(Figure 10.49)**.

3. With the Message Composition window active in Netscape, choose Paste as Quotation in the Edit menu **(Fig. 10.50)**. The copied text will be pasted with a greater than sign at the beginning of each line **(Fig. 10.51)**.

✔ **Tip**

■ Netscape actually inserts a greater than sign (the Internet-recognized symbol for quoted text) at the beginning of each *paragraph*. Since most electronic mail is made up of one-line paragraphs, this system works fine for quoting from messages. If you paste text from other programs, you may notice that there is only one greater than sign at the beginning of each paragraph. In this case, either insert the additional symbols manually, or copy each line individually.

Forwarding a message

Sometimes you will receive e-mail that either isn't for you or that you would like to share with others. The easiest way to share mail you have received with other people is to forward it.

To forward a message as an attachment:

1. Select the message that you wish to forward in the Mail window **(Figure 10.52)**. The contents of the message appear in the lower pane.

2. Select Forward in the Message menu **(Fig. 10.53)**. The Message Composition window appears. The Subject is automatically set to "[Fwd: title of original message]" and the original message is attached to the new message.

3. Enter the recipient's address in the Mail To box.

4. Fill in the other message parts as desired.

5. Add any personal comments about the forwarded material in the message area.

6. Click the Send button or choose the Send command in the File menu.

✔ Tips

■ You can also click the Forward button on the toolbar to forward a message **(Figure 10.54)**

■ A forwarded message appears below the main message, much like an attached document **(Figure 10.55)**.

■ You can forward news postings to yourself to keep a record of them.

Figure 10.52 *Choose the message you wish to forward.*

Figure 10.53 *Choose Forward in the Message menu.*

Figure 10.54 *Or, click the Forward button.*

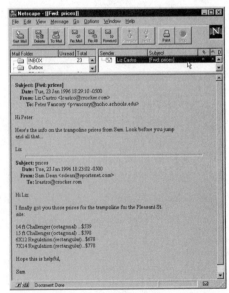

Figure 10.55 *A forwarded message appears below the new portion of the current message.*

Figure 10.56 *Choose Forward Quoted in the Message menu.*

Figure 10.57 *The forwarded message appears as a quote (with >) in the contents area.*

Figure 10.58 *Type the new material below the quoted message.*

Figure 10.59 *The original message appears as a quote in the new message.*

Forwarding a message as a quote

You can also forward a message as a quote, that is with greater than signs (>) at the beginning of each line.

To forward a message as a quote:

1. Select the message that you wish to forward in the Mail window. The contents of the message appear in the lower pane.

2. Select Forward Quoted in the Message menu **(Figure 10.56)**. The Message Composition window appears. The Subject is automatically set to "[Fwd: title of original message]" and the original message is quoted in the message area **(Figure 10.57)**.

3. Enter the recipient's address in the Mail To box.

4. Fill in the other message parts as desired.

5. Add any personal comments about the forwarded material in the message area below the quoted, forwarded message **(Figure 10.58)**.

6. Click the Send button, or choose the Send command in the File menu.

Forwarding a message as a quote

Attaching files to a message

Electronic mail does not limit you to letters; you can send packages, too. You can attach any kind of file to a message—including images or even programs. You can also attach a URL to a message, giving the recipient direct access to a Web page *(see page 127)*.

To attach a file to a message:

1. Choose New Mail Message in the File menu or select a message and choose Reply in the Message menu. The Message Composition window appears.

2. Choose Attach File in the File menu **(Figure 10.60)** or click the Attach button.

3. In the Attachments dialog box that appears, click Attach File **(Fig. 10.61)**.

4. In the dialog box that appears, select the file that you wish to send with the message and click Open **(Fig. 10.62)**.

5. In the Attachments dialog box that reappears, choose As Is to send the file in its current form or choose Convert to Plain Text to send the file as text **(Figure 10.63)**.

6. Click OK. The file's path appears in the Attachments box in the Message Composition window **(Fig. 10.64)**.

7. Compose the rest of the message.

✔ Tip

■ Click the Attach button to add or edit an attached file.

Figure 10.60 *From the Message Composition window, choose Attach File in the File menu.*

Figure 10.61 *Click the Attach File button in the Attachments dialog box.*

Figure 10.62 *Choose the desired file and click Open.*

Figure 10.63 *The selected file appears in the Attachments dialog box. Click As is or Convert to Plain Text and then click OK.*

Figure 10.64 *The attached file appears in the Attachment field in the Message Composition window.*

Figure 10.65
Click Attach Location (URL) in the Attachments dialog box.

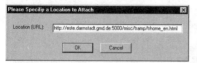

Figure 10.66 *Type or paste the URL and click OK.*

Figure 10.67
The URL appears in the Attachments dialog box. Click As Is to send it with HTML tags and Convert to plain text to send it without.

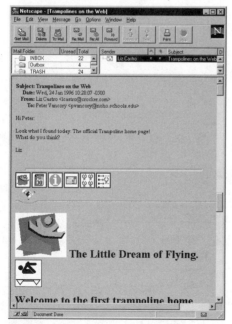

Figure 10.68 *As long as the recipient views the message with Netscape, the URL appears within the message just like any other Web page.*

Attaching a URL to a message

If you find a great Web page on the Net and want to share it with someone, instead of sending the page's address in text form, you can send them the actual page within your message. As long as they use Netscape to view your message, the page will appear just as if they had jumped to it themselves **(Figure 10.68)**.

To attach a URL to a message:

1. From the Message Composition window, choose Attach File or click the Attach button.

2. In the Attachments dialog that appears, click Attach Location (URL) **(Figure 10.65)**.

3. Type or paste the desired URL in the dialog box that appears and click OK **(Figure 10.66)**.

4. In the Attachments dialog box, choose As Is to send the page with HTML tags; choose Convert to Plain Text to send it without **(Fig. 10.67)**. For more information about tags, consult *Saving a Web page* on page 54.

5. Repeat steps 3–5 for each URL you wish to attach.

6. Click OK to close the dialog box. The URL appears in the Attachments box in the Message Composition window.

7. Compose the rest of the message as usual *(see page 115)*.

✔ Tip

■ If you're not sure what program the recipient uses for e-mail, send the page without tags.

Attaching a URL to a message

Mailing a document

Earlier versions of Netscape allowed you to mail a Web page directly from the browser. Although Netscape's mail features have expanded, the old command remains. The effect is virtually identical to attaching a URL *(see page 127)*. The only difference is that the actual URL, as a link, is added to the note above the page itself.

To mail a document:

1. In the browser, jump to or open the desired Web page.

2. Choose Mail Document in the File menu **(Figure 10.69)**. The Message Composition window appears with the Web page automatically attached and the URL as a link in the body of the message **(Figure 10.70)**.

3. Edit and send the message as usual *(see page 115)*. The mailed document appears both as a link and as an attachment to the recipient **(Figure 10.71)**.

✔ Tip

■ You can also mail an individual frame. Simply select the frame and the Mail Document command turns into Mail Frame in the File menu.

Figure 10.69 *Jump to (or open) the desired page and select Mail Document in the File menu.*

Figure 10.70 *The page's URL is attached and added to the contents of the message. Add the name and contents and send as usual.*

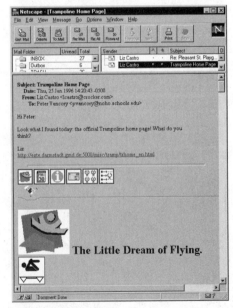

Figure 10.71 *The link to the page and the page itself appear below the message.*

Mailing a document

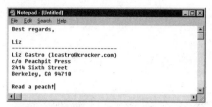

Figure 10.72 *A signature typically contains your name, e-mail and snail mail addresses, and a pithy quote. This one was created with Notepad.*

Figure 10.73 *Choose Save As in the text editor's File menu.*

Figure 10.74 *Save the signature file as a Text File (*.TXT).*

Creating a signature file

One of the nice traditions of e-mail writing is adding a few lines at the bottom of the note that tell who you are, and sometimes what you do and where you're from. You can set Netscape up to add these few lines, called a *signature*, to all your outgoing correspondence. You can create a signature in any word processor, including Notepad or Wordpad.

To create a signature:

1. Open a word processor or text editor. Write, Notepad or WordPad are fine.

2. Create your signature as desired **(Figure 10.72)**. A signature typically contains your name, e-mail and snail mail addresses, and a pithy quote. You can also add ASCII images.

3. Choose Save As in the text editor's File menu **(Figure 10.73)**.

4. Give the file a name and choose the Text (*.TXT) format in the Save As dialog box. Click Save **(Fig. 10.74)**.

5. To use the signature file, consult *Using a signature file* on page 130.

✔ Tip

- Although a signature is limited to text characters, you can be creative about how to use them. Some people even make pictures out of text characters, others simply add famous quotes and sayings to their signatures.

Creating a signature file

Using a signature file

Once you've created a signature file *(see page 129)*, Netscape can automatically add it to each message that you send. All you have to do is tell Netscape where the signature file is.

To use a signature file:

1. In Netscape, choose Mail and News Preferences in the Options menu **(Figure 10.75)**.

2. In the Preferences dialog box that appears, click the Identity tab **(Figure 10.76)**.

3. At the bottom of the Identity preferences tab, click Browse.

4. Choose the desired signature file in the dialog box that appears and click Open **(Figure 10.77)**. The file's path will appear in the Identity preferences tab **(Figure 10.78)**.

5. Click OK to close the Identity tab. The next time you write a message, Netscape will include your signature automatically **(Figure 10.79)**.

✔ Tips

■ If the signature file does not appear in the Open dialog box when you try to choose it, you probably didn't save it in Text Only (or ASCII) format *(see page 129)*.

■ If you move the signature file, or change its name or the name of the folder it's in, Netscape won't be able to find it and will simply stop adding it to your messages. Unfortunately, Netscape won't tell you there's a problem, so you have to watch it.

Figure 10.75 *Choose Mail and News Preferences in the Options menu.*

Figure 10.76 *Click the Identity tab and then the Browse button to choose a signature file.*

Figure 10.77 *Choose the desired signature file and click Open.*

Figure 10.78 *The path to the selected signature file now appears in the Identity preferences tab.*

Figure 10.79 *The signature file is automatically copied to each new Message Composition window.*

Using a signature file

The Address Book

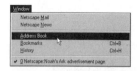

Figure 11.1 *Choose Address Book in the Window menu to open the Address Book.*

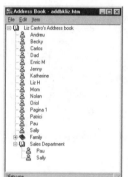

Figure 11.2
The Address Book helps you keep track of those long and complicated e-mail addresses.

The Address Book window

Netscape lets you save e-mail addresses in the Address Book, a window that you can let float on the screen beside the main Netscape window or hide at your convenience.

The Address Book includes not only the e-mail addresses themselves, but also the recipient's name, a description, and a nickname if desired. The Address Book always lists addresses by their names in alphabetical order.

An address book can also contain *mailing lists* that make it easy to send messages to more than one person at a time. Because a mailing list is actually a collection of *aliases* of addresses and not the addresses themselves, you can include an address in as many mailing lists as desired.

To open the Address Book:

Choose Address Book in the Window menu **(Figure 11.1)**. The Address Book appears **(Figure 11.2)**.

The Address Book window

Adding an address

E-mail addresses tend to be long and hard to remember. You can store e-mail addresses in an address book together with the recipient's name, a description, and a nickname.

To add an address to the Address Book:

1. Open the Address Book window by choosing Address Book in the Window menu.

2. Choose Add User in the Item menu **(Figure 11.3)**. The Address Properties dialog box appears.

3. Enter a short, descriptive, easy-to-remember word for the Nickname **(Figure 11.4)**. You can use the nickname to call up the person's name and e-mail address in a message.

4. Enter the Name of the person or organization that corresponds to the e-mail address. The Name will appear on all correspondence that you send out, and it will identify the incoming and outgoing mail in the Mail window.

5. In the E-mail Address field, type the e-mail address carefully. One mistyped digit or letter can keep your mail from getting to its destination.

6. If desired, enter a description for the address in the Description field.

7. Click OK. The address appears in the Address book in alphabetical order **(Figure 11.5)**.

✔ Complaint

■ Netscape uses "Nick Name" as some sort of tribute to Mr. Nolte. But, in my book, *Nickname* is just one word.

Figure 11.3 *In the Address Book, choose Add User in the Item menu.*

Figure 11.4 *The Address Book dialog appears, in which you can enter the desired information.*

Figure 11.5 *The new address appears in the Address Book window.*

Adding an address

Figure 11.6 *Select the letter from the person whose address you wish to add to your Address Book.*

Figure 11.7 *Choose Add to Address Book in the Mail window's Message menu.*

Figure 11.8 *The sender's name and e-mail address are entered in the Address Book dialog box automatically. Enter a nickname and description, if desired, and click OK.*

Figure 11.9 *The new address appears in the Address Book.*

Adding an address from incoming messages

You can add the address of anyone who has sent you a message. Adding an address in this way ensures that the address is not misspelled.

To add an address from incoming messages:

1. Open the message from which you wish to copy the sender's address **(Figure 11.6)**.

2. Choose Add to Address Book in the Message menu **(Figure 11.7)**. The Address Book dialog box appears with the name and address automatically filled in.

3. Add a nickname and description if desired **(Figure 11.8)**. For more information, consult *Adding an address* on page 132.

4. Click OK. The new address is added to your address book **(Figure 11.9)**.

✔ Tips

■ It is possible (and not very hard, as you can see by Figure 11.6) to send mail with a false address. If the sender has not used a real address, you won't be able to use it to write them back.

■ You can add addresses from news postings using this same technique.

Adding an address from incoming messages

Creating a mailing list

The Address Book lets you create a mailing list, similar to the aliases in the Bookmarks window, that lets you send e-mail messages to a whole group of people at the same time.

To create a mailing list:

1. Open the Address Book by choosing Address Book in the Window menu.

2. Choose Add List in the Item menu (**Figure 11.10**). The Address Book dialog box appears.

3. Enter a short, descriptive, easy-to-remember word for the Nickname (**Figure 11.11**). You will be able to use the nickname to invoke the list.

4. Type a name for the mailing list in the Name field. A mailing list's name is like a nickname for *all of the addresses* the list contains. As such, it does not appear on any of your correspondence but instead is replaced by the addresses of each person on the list.

5. In the Description field, type a few words that define the list's members.

6. Click OK to save the changes.

7. Select the addresses that you wish to add to the mailing list (**Fig. 11.12**).

8. Drag the names to the new list's icon. Aliases of the addresses are added to the new list while the addresses themselves remain unchanged and in their original positions (**Figure 11.13**).

✔ Tip

■ You can add more names to the mailing list at any time. Simply drag them on top of the list's icon as in step 8.

Figure 11.10 *In the Address Book, choose Add List in the Item menu.*

Figure 11.11 *In the Address Book dialog box, enter the nickname, name, and description for the mailing list.*

Figure 11.12 *Select the addresses you wish to add to the mailing list. Use Shift to add multiple, sequential addresses. Use Control to add non-sequential ones. Then drag the selection to the new mailing list.*

Figure 11.13 *The new mailing list appears in the Address Book with its contents below. Double click the list's icon to hide (or show) its addresses.*

Figure 11.14 *In the Address Book, select the desired address by clicking it once. Select additional addresses with Shift (if they're touching in the list) or Control (if they're not).*

Figure 11.15 *Choose Mail New Message in the File menu.*

Figure 11.16 *A pre-addressed Message Composition window appears.*

Using an address or list

The beauty of the Address Book is that you can send e-mail to someone without having to type his address. A list lets you e-mail *several* people at once.

To use an address or list:

1. Select the desired address or list in the Address Book **(Figure 11.14)**.

2. Choose Mail New Message in the File menu **(Figure 11.15)**. The Message Composition window appears, automatically addressed to the person or list of people selected in step 1 **(Figure 11.16)**.

3. Compose the message as usual.

✔ Tips

■ You can double click an address to open a new, automatically addressed Message Composition window.

■ Once in the Message Composition window, click any of the address buttons (Mail to, Cc, etc.) to access the Address Book.

■ You can also type a nickname in a field in the Message Composition window to add an address or list to that field. When you press the Tab key (to go to the next field), the nickname is replaced by the full address.

Changing or deleting an address or list

You may need to change an entry in your address book, for example, if the person changes online services, or to add descriptive information or a nickname.

To change an address or list:

1. Click once on the address or list to select it and then choose Properties in the Item menu **(Figure 11.17)**.

2. In the Address Book dialog box that appears, change the values in the fields as desired **(Figure 11.18 and Figure 11.19)**.

3. Click OK to save the changes.

Getting rid of unused addresses or lists is simple and essential. The cleaner you keep your address book, the easier it will be to find the addresses you *do* use.

To delete an address or list:

1. Select the item you wish to delete in the Address Book by clicking it once.

2. Choose Delete in the Edit menu in the Address Book window, or press the Delete key—not the Backspace key **(Figure 11.20)**. The address or list disappears.

✔ Tip

■ No alert appears when you delete an address or list, unless the item has an alias. If you delete an item by mistake, choose Undo immediately to restore it.

Figure 11.17
Select the address or list that you wish to change. Then choose Properties in the Item menu.

Figure 11.18 *If you've selected an individual address, the Address dialog box appears. Edit the address as desired.*

Figure 11.19 *If you've selected a list to change, an almost identical Address Book dialog box appears in which to make the changes. The only field you can't change (of course) is the E-mail Address field.*

Figure 11.20 *Choose Delete in the Address Book's Edit menu or press the Delete key (not Backspace).*

Figure 11.21
Choose Find in the Address Book's Edit menu.

Figure 11.22 *Type the search criteria and click OK.*

Figure 11.23
Netscape highlights the first address that satisfies the criteria. Why is this address highlighted? Check out Figure 11.24.

Figure 11.24 *The address found in Figure 11.23 contained the search criteria in its Description field.*

Figure 11.25 *To find the next address that satisfies the criteria, choose Find again in the Address Book's window.*

Figure 11.26
The next address that contains the search criteria (this time in the Name itself) is highlighted.

Finding an address or list

If you have many entries in your address book, it may be hard to find just the address you're looking for. You can search the contents of the Address Book to find the information you need quickly.

To find an address:

1. Choose Find in the Address Book's Edit menu **(Figure 11.21)**.

2. In the dialog box that appears, type the text that you wish to search for and click OK **(Figure 11.22)**. Netscape highlights the first entry that satisfies the search criteria **(Figure 11.23)**.

3. If the selected address is not the one you're looking for, choose Find Again in the Address Book's Edit menu **(Figure 11.25)**. The next entry that satisfies the search criteria is highlighted **(Figure 11.26)**.

4. Repeat step 3 until you've found the desired address.

✔ Tip

■ Netscape searches in each of the fields in each address. If it's not obvious why a certain address has been highlighted, it's probably because the search criteria was found in one of the fields that is not directly visible from the Address Book window—like Nickname, E-mail Address, or Description **(Figure 11.24)**.

Finding an address or list

Saving an address book

You can save an address book in order to share it with others or simply to make a back-up copy. In fact, an address book is nothing more than an HTML page that you can browse as you would any other local file.

Figure 11.27
Choose Save As in the Address Book's File menu.

To save an address book:

1. Choose Save As in the Address Book's File menu **(Figure 11.27)**. The Save dialog box appears **(Fig. 11.28)**.

2. Give the file a name and choose the directory in which to save it.

3. Choose a file type for the address book. If you want to open the file with Netscape, choose HTML Files. To open the file in a word processor or text editor, choose Plain Text (*.txt).

4. Click Save to save the file.

Figure 11.28 *In the Save dialog box, give the Address Book file a name, choose HTML Files (to save it with HTML tags) or Text (to save it without HTML tags) and then click OK.*

✔ Tips

■ If you save the address book in HTML Files format, Netscape automatically adds the extension .htm to the end of the address book's name, so that you'll be able to open the file as a regular Web page *(see page 140)*. Each of the addresses in the address book is converted into a link on the Web page.

■ Yes, the title of the dialog box that appears is Save *bookmarks* file, but it works fine with address books, too.

Saving an address book

Figure 11.29
Choose Import in the Address Book's File menu.

Figure 11.30 *Select the desired address book file and click Open.*

Figure 11.31 *The new addresses are added to the existing ones in the Address Book window. Addresses with the same names are not replaced, simply added.*

Importing an address book

You can import the addresses from a saved address book file into your current address book. For example, you can save the address book file on your computer at work and then import it into your address book at your home computer.

To import an address book:

1. Choose Import in the Address Book's File menu **(Figure 11.29)**. The Import dialog box appears.

2. If desired, choose HTML Files in the List Files of Type menu. Only files in HTML format, like address books, will be visible in the dialog box.

3. Choose the address book file that you wish to import and click Open **(Figure 11.30)**. The addresses in the imported file are displayed in the current Address Book window **(Figure 11.31)**.

✔ Tips

■ Currently, Netscape does not replace or update names that already exist. It simply adds the new entries. The only unique part of an address is the nickname. If an incoming address has the same nickname as an existing address, the incoming address' nickname will be lost.

■ Yes, the name of the dialog box that appears is Import *bookmarks* file, but it works just fine with addresses.

Importing an address book

Opening an address book as a Web page

An easy way to see an address book without changing your regular address book is to open it as a Web page. Since the address book is in HTML format, like any other Web page, Netscape knows how to interpret it correctly, displaying all the addresses as links which can be clicked on to send a message to the corresponding person.

To open an address book as a Web page:

1. Save your address book, making sure to choose HTML Files in the List Files of Type pop-up menu. For more information, consult *Saving an address book* on page 138.

2. Choose Open File in the File menu in the main Netscape window **(Figure 11.32)**.

3. Choose the desired file and click Open **(Figure 11.33)**. The address book file is loaded into Netscape and each address is automatically converted into a link **(Fig. 11.34)**.

✔ Tip

■ You can use this technique to create a Web page that elicits feedback from your readers. Save an address book that contains all of the public relations or technical support people in your company. Then include the address book cum Web page in your site. Your readers will have instant e-mail access to all of the people in the address book.

Figure 11.32 *In the main Netscape File menu, choose Open File.*

Figure 11.33 *In the Open dialog box, choose the desired address book file that you wish to open.*

Figure 11.34 *An Address Book file opened as a Web page appears with each address as a link. Users can click the address to send a message to the corresponding person. (This isn't my real Address Book, I confess.)*

The News Window

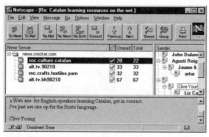

Figure 12.1 *The upper left pane (enlarged here) lists the news hosts and available newsgroups.*

Figure 12.2 *When you click a newsgroup, its postings are displayed in the upper right pane of the News window (enlarged here).*

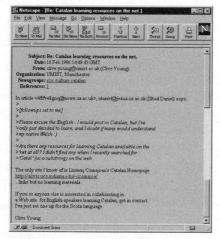

Figure 12.3 *A click on a posting reveals the message in the lower pane (enlarged here).*

The News window is Netscape's central command area for displaying the newsgroups available through your server and the postings that belong to each one. From the News window, you can view and subscribe to newsgroups, and read and reply to postings or create your own.

There is an enormous amount of traffic in the newsgroups. The News window lets you flag postings that are important and mark an individual posting, a thread, or even an entire newsgroup as read, so that it doesn't appear the next time you view the newsgroup.

The parts of the News window

The News window is divided into three areas, or panes. The top left panel **(Figure 12.1)** lists the newsgroups, and gives the number of unread and total messages in each, and tells whether you're subscribed. You can choose to view *all* the newsgroups, the *new* newsgroups, only the newsgroups you've *subscribed to,* or only the newsgroups you've subscribed to that *have new messages.*

When you click one of the newsgroups, a list of the postings it contains appears in the top right pane of the News window **(Figure 12.2)**. Each posting is identified by its Subject, Sender, Date, and whether it has been marked or read.

Once you click a posting, the contents of the message appears in the bottom pane of the News window **(Figure 12.3)**.

The parts of the News window

Using the News window

The most important difference between the News window and the Mail window is that the former shows newsgroups and postings while the latter shows folders and e-mail. Overall, however, their functions are virtually identical:

To get around in the News window, consult *Navigating through your messages* on page 114.

To resize the News window and its individual panes, consult *Changing the size of the panes* on page 106. To resize the columns or change their order, consult *Changing the columns* on page 107. To change the layout of the window, consult *The parts of the Mail window* on page 91

To choose a font for viewing News messages, consult *Changing your messages' appearance* on page 108.

To sort your postings, consult *Putting your messages in order* on page 102. To view your postings in hierarchical order, instead of strictly by date or sender, consult *Threading messages* on page 105.

To open the News window:

Choose Netscape News in the Window menu **(Figure 12.4)**. The News window is displayed with the news host (if any) listed in the top left pane. (For more information about news hosts, consult *Opening a news host* on page 144.)

To close the News window:

Click the close box in the upper right window of the News window or double click the News icon in the upper left corner of the News window **(Figure 12.5 and Figure 12.6)**.

Figure 12.4 *Choose Netscape News in the Window menu to open the News window.*

Figure 12.5 *Click the standard Window buttons to adjust the window. From left to right: Minimize, Maximize and Close.*

Figure 12.6 *Or double click the Netscape news icon in the upper left corner to close the News window.*

Figure 12.7 *A news host may offer several different categories of newsgroups. Click a plus sign to
see the individual newsgroups in each section.*

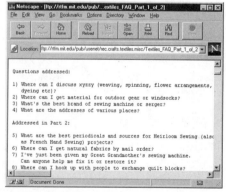

Figure 12.8 *A FAQ (this one is from the newsgroup* rec.crafts.textiles*) tells what topics are discussed in a particular newsgroup and gives
general information about those topics.*

Where newsgroup names come from

There are several major categories of
newsgroups: alt (*alternative*, includes a
wide variety of groups from alt.sex to
alt.appalachian), comp (*computer*, with
every program and operating system
imaginable), news (*newsgroups*, most
contain information about newsgroups
themselves), rec (*recreation*, from
rec.arts.cinema to rec.games.go to
rec.sport.fencing), sci (*science*, from sci.
archaeology to sci.virtual-worlds), and soc
(*society*, includes the soc.culture newsgroups that discuss different countries and
their customs). Your server will probably
have access to several more categories,
including specialty or local groups.

One good way to find out what a newsgroup is about is by reading its FAQ or *frequently asked questions* file, if it has one.
Each newsgroup's FAQ is generally
posted to the newsgroup once a month.
You can find many of them at **ftp://
rtfm.mit.edu/pub/usenet/newsgroup.
name** where *newsgroup.name* is the full
name of the newsgroup in question.

Where newsgroup names come from

Opening a news host

Most people have access to only one news server or host. In general, the news host's name is *news.service-provider-name.com* (or .edu). If you're not sure, contact your Internet service provider. You must open at least one news host so that Netscape knows where to connect to get the data for the newsgroups.

To open a new newsgroup host:

1. With the News window active, choose Open News Host in the File menu **(Figure 12.9)**.

2. In the dialog box that appears, type the name of your news server—something like **news.provider.com**. Consult your Internet provider if you're not sure **(Figure 12.10)**.

3. Click OK. Netscape contacts the news host and, if you have the proper access privileges, shows the news host folder in the left pane of the News window **(Figure 12.11)**.

✔ Tips

■ Some news hosts restrict access to certain users. Others let anyone connect to see the newsgroups it contains. For example, to see the newsgroups offered to the public by Netscape Communications, open the news host **secnews.netscape.com**. (The name of the Netscape newsgroup is **netscape.navigator**.)

■ You can open as many news hosts as you have access to.

■ To eliminate a news host, select it and choose Remove News Host in the File menu **(Figure 12.12)**. The news host disappears.

Figure 12.9 *Choose Open News Host in the File menu to set up a new newsgroup server.*

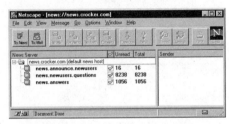

Figure 12.10 *In the dialog box that appears, type the name of the news host (generally "news" followed by the server name).*

Figure 12.11 *The news host appears in the upper left pane of the News window. Sometimes there will already be a few newsgroups showing, but usually you'll have to download the whole list (see page 145).*

Figure 12.12 *To eliminate an old or unused news host from the left pane, choose Remove News Host in the File menu.*

Opening a news host

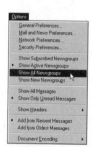

Figure 12.13 *Select the news host and click the plus sign next to its name to open it.*

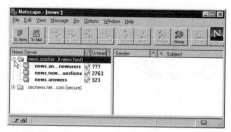

Figure 12.14 *Choose Show All Newsgroups in the Options menu.*

Figure 12.15 *All of the newsgroups that the news host contains are displayed, divided into categories. Click the plus sign next to a newsgroup folder (which has an asterisk in its name) to see the newsgroups it contains.*

Getting a list of all newsgroups

Your Internet service provider decides which newsgroups you have access to and which you don't. Some commercial online services like CompuServe and AOL have gotten a bit of press lately about their efforts to censor certain newsgroups. By downloading the full list from the server, you can see exactly what you get. It also makes it easy to browse through them and subscribe to the ones that interest you *(see page 149)*.

To get a list of all newsgroups:

1. Select a news host and then click the plus sign next to the news host's name to open it **(Figure 12.13)**.

2. Choose Show All Newsgroups in the Options menu **(Figure 12.14)**. If this is the first time that you've selected this option with this news host, it may take a few minutes. All of the available newsgroups are listed in the upper left pane **(Figure 12.15)**.

✔ Tips

■ Viewing all the newsgroups is useful for finding new newsgroups. You can then create a subset of newsgroups that interest you and hide the rest. For more information on choosing a subset, consult *Subscribing to a newsgroup* on page 149. For more details on hiding the newsgroups that don't interest you, consult *Showing only subscribed newsgroups* on page 150.

■ Click the plus sign next to a name with an asterisk to see all the newsgroups in that category. Click the minus sign to hide them.

Getting a list of all newsgroups

Getting a list of new newsgroups

New newsgroups are created all the time. All it takes is a group of people who write a charter, elicit votes from the potential public, and then distribute the new newsgroups to the Internet. You can search for and display the newsgroups which have been added since the last time you checked.

To get a list of new newsgroups:

1. Select the desired news host and click the plus sign to its left.

2. With the News window active, choose Show New Newsgroups in the Options menu **(Figure 12.16)**. A message will appear that tells you how many new newsgroups have been added, if any, since the last time you used this command.

3. Click OK **(Figure 12.17 and Figure 12.18)**. The new newsgroups are displayed at the end of the current newsgroup list **(Figure 12.19)**.

✔ Tip

■ You are not automatically subscribed to new newsgroups. For more information on subscribing, consult *Subscribing to a newsgroup* on page 149.

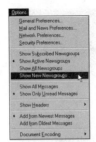

Figure 12.16 *With the News window active, choose Show New Newsgroups in the Options menu.*

Figure 12.17 *Netscape will show an alert if no newsgroups have been created since the last time you checked.*

Figure 12.18 *If new newsgroups have been created since the last time you checked, Netscape will tell you how many there are and then display them at the bottom of the current list.*

Figure 12.19 *Netscape lists the new newsgroup (sci.med.diseases.als) at the end of your current list. You are not automatically subscribed to it.*

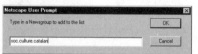

Figure 12.20 *With the News window active, choose Add Newsgroup in the File menu.*

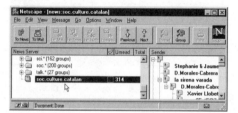

Figure 12.21 *In the dialog box that appears, type the full name of the newsgroup that you want to view.*

Figure 12.22 *The new newsgroup appears at the end of the list in the left pane. You are not automatically subscribed to it.*

Viewing a newsgroup by name

If you know the name of a newsgroup, you don't have to sort through the full list in order to view it.

To view a newsgroup when you know its name:

1. With the News window active, choose Add Newsgroup in the File menu **(Figure 12.20)**.

2. In the dialog box that appears, type the full name of the newsgroup that you want to view **(Figure 12.21)**.

3. Click OK. The newsgroup appears in the left pane of the News window **(Figure 12.22)**.

✔ Tip

■ The newsgroup will disappear from the list when you close the News window unless you subscribe to it. You are not automatically subscribed to a newsgroup when you view it. For more information, consult *Subscribing to a newsgroup* on page 149.

Viewing a newsgroup by name

Viewing a newsgroup from other windows

You can view, and then subscribe to, a newsgroup from the browser or the Mail window. If you know the newsgroup's name, you can type it in the Location field in the browser. In addition, if you encounter a link to the newsgroup, either on a Web page or in an e-mail message, you can click the link to view the newsgroup.

To use the Location field in the browser to view a newsgroup:

1. In the main Netscape window, type **news:newsgroup.address** in the Location field, where *newsgroup.address* is the complete name of the newsgroup that you wish to view **(Figure 12.23)**. Netscape automatically displays the News window with the selected newsgroup at the bottom of the list in the left pane.

2. Click the newsgroup's name to display the messages in the right pane of the News window **(Figure 12.24)**.

To jump to a newsgroup from a Web page or e-mail:

1. Click the link on the Web page or e-mail message **(Figure 12.25)**. The News window opens and displays the newsgroup in the left pane.

2. Click the newsgroup's name to view its messages in the right pane **(Figure 12.26)**.

✔ Tip

■ You are not automatically subscribed to a newsgroup when you view it *(see page 149)*.

Figure 12.23 *Type* **news:** *followed by the newsgroup's name in the Location field in the main Netscape window.*

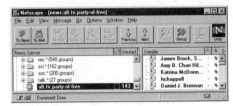

Figure 12.24 *The newsgroup appears at the bottom of the list and its messages appear in the right pane.*

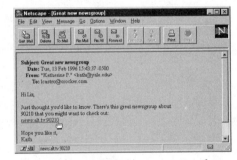

Figure 12.25 *Click a link to a newsgroup from a Web page or an e-mail message.*

Figure 12.26 *Netscape automatically switches to the News window and shows the newsgroup in the left pane at the bottom of the list with its messages in the right pane.*

Figure 12.27 *Scroll around in the list of newsgroups in the left pane until you see the one that you want to subscribe to. Click the plus sign next to folders to open them (or click the minus sign to hide their contents).*

Figure 12.28 *Click the box next to the newsgroup's name to subscribe to it. A yellow checkmark will appear.*

Subscribing to a newsgroup

You can browse through the postings in any newsgroup from the full list *(see page 145)*. However, since there are over 14,000 individual newsgroups, it is handy to select a few that you wish to follow—which will appear each time you open the News window—and hide the rest. Selecting a newsgroup is called *subscribing* to it.

To subscribe to a newsgroup:

1. Use the techniques described on the preceding pages to show the desired newsgroup in the upper left pane of the News window **(Figure 12.27)**.

2. Click in the Subscribed column (the one headed by ✓), directly to the right of the newsgroup's name **(Figure 12.28)**. A yellow checkmark appears next to the newsgroup to show that you have subscribed to it.

To cancel a subscription to a newsgroup:

Click the yellow checkmark next to a newsgroup's name to cancel a subscription. The yellow checkmark disappears.

✔ Tip

■ You can subscribe to as many newsgroups as you like. The idea, of course, is to subscribe to the ones that you will actually read, and then hide the rest. You can always go back to the main list.

Subscribing to a newsgroup

149

Showing only subscribed newsgroups

Once you have subscribed to each newsgroup in which you are interested, you can hide the rest. You can also choose to view only the newsgroups to which you are subscribed that have new messages (since the last time you checked).

To show only the newsgroups that you have subscribed to:

1. Select a news host in the News window.

2. Choose Show Subscribed Newsgroups in the Options menu **(Figure 12.29)**. The extra newsgroups are hidden and only the newsgroups that you have subscribed to are shown **(Figure 12.30)**.

Some of the newsgroups to which you have subscribed may have many new messages added each day. Others may not see any action during weeks. You can choose to display only those newsgroups to which you have subscribed that have *new* messages.

To show only the newsgroups with new messages:

1. Select a news host in the News window.

2. Choose Show Active Newsgroups in the Options menu **(Figure 12.31)**. Only the newsgroups to which you are subscribed that have new messages are displayed **(Figure 12.32)**.

Figure 12.29 *With the News window open, choose Show Subscribed Newsgroups in the Options menu.*

Figure 12.30 *Only the newsgroups that you have subscribed to (marked by a yellow checkmark) are shown in the left pane of the News window.*

Figure 12.31 *With the News window active, choose Show Active Newsgroups in the Options menu.*

Figure 12.32 *Netscape only shows those newsgroups that you're subscribed to that have messages that you haven't read yet. (Notice that the rec.crafts.textiles.yarn newsgroup that appeared in Figure 12.30 does not appear here, because it has no unread messages.)*

Showing only subscribed newsgroups

Figure 12.33 *The new unread messages appear in bold face with a green diamond.*

Figure 12.34 *After selecting the desired message(s), choose Mark as Read in the Message menu.*

Figure 12.35 *The message marked as read is no longer shown in bold face, and loses its diamond.*

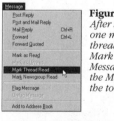

Figure 12.36
After selecting any one message in the thread, choose Mark Thread Read in the Message menu (left) or click the Mark Thread button on the toolbar (right).

Figure 12.37 *All the messages in the thread are marked as read and, as such, are shown in plain text without the green diamond.*

Marking messages as read

If you don't have enough time to read every message, or if you can tell by the subject line which messages are of interest, you can mark these messages as read so that they don't appear the next time you open that newsgroup.

To mark messages as read:

1. Select the messages that you wish to mark as read **(Figure 12.33)**.

2. Choose Mark as Read or Mark as Unread in the Message menu **(Figure 12.34)**. Read messages no longer appear in boldface, nor do they carry a green diamond **(Figure 12.35)**.

To mark a thread as read:

1. Select a message in the thread. You don't need to select all of them.

2. Choose Mark Thread Read in the Message menu **(Figure 12.36)**. The messages in the thread no longer appear in boldface, nor do they have a green diamond **(Figure 12.37)**.

✔ Tips

■ You can hide read messages. For more information, consult *Hiding read messages* on page 153.

■ You can also click the Mark Thread button on the toolbar to mark a thread as read. Click the green diamond next to any message to mark it as read. Click it again to mark it as unread.

■ For more information about threaded messages, consult *Threading messages* on page 105.

Marking messages as read

Marking an entire newsgroup as read

Sometimes you'll want to mark an entire newsgroup as read so that the next time you open the newsgroup you'll be sure that the messages are new.

To mark an entire newsgroup as read:

1. Select the newsgroup—or any message in the newsgroup—that you wish to mark as read **(Figure 12.38)**.

2. Choose Mark Newsgroup Read in the Message menu **(Figure 12.39)**. All the messages in the newsgroup are marked as read **(Figure 12.40)**.

✔ Tip

■ You can also click the Mark Group button on the toolbar to mark a group as read **(Figure 12.41)**.

Figure 12.38 *Choose a newsgroup that you wish to mark as read. (You can also click a message within the newsgroup.)*

Figure 12.39 *Select Mark Newsgroup Read in the Message menu.*

Figure 12.40 *All the messages in the newsgroup are marked as read, and are shown in plain text without the green diamond.*

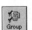 **Figure 12.41** *You can also click the Mark Group button to mark a newsgroup as read.*

Figure 12.42 *When you read a message or mark it as read, the boldface lettering and green diamond disappear.*

Figure 12.43 *Choose Show Only Unread Messages to hide the messages you've read or marked as read.*

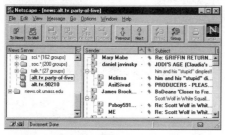

Figure 12.44 *Only the unread messages are shown.*

Figure 12.45 *Choose Show All Messages in the Options menu to view both the read and unread messages.*

Hiding read messages

Once you've read a message, you can make it disappear so that it's easier to find the messages you *haven't* read yet.

To hide read messages:

Choose Show Only Unread Messages in the Options menu **(Figure 12.43)**. The messages that you've read—or marked as read—disappear **(Figure 12.44)**.

To show both read and unread messages:

Choose Show All Messages in the Options menu **(Figure 12.45)**. Both the messages that you've read as well as those you haven't appear in the right pane.

✔ Tip

■ If you had already selected Show Only Unread Messages in the Options menu, and then read a few messages, the messages don't disappear as you read them. In fact, selecting the option again has no effect. First, you have to select Show All Messages and *then* choose Show Only Unread Messages. Seems like a bug to me.

Hiding read messages

Getting more messages

Although some newsgroups can contain hundreds or even thousands of messages at a time, Netscape will only load a certain number of these to start. For example, the newsgroup may contain 1,238 messages, but Newsgroup will load only 100 at a time. Once you're through with the first one hundred, you can load in more.

To get more messages:

1. Select the desired newsgroup (or any message that it contains) **(Fig. 12.46)**.

2. Choose Get More Messages in the File menu **(Fig. 12.47)**. Netscape displays the new set of messages **(Fig. 12.48)**.

To change the number of messages loaded at a time:

1. Choose Mail and News Preferences in the Options menu. The Preferences box appears. Click the Server tab.

2. Type a new number in the text box next to Get xx Messages at a Time (Max 3500) **(Figure 12.49)**.

3. Click OK to close the dialog box.

✔ Tips

■ While your postings may be in order of Sender or Subject, the new postings shown are chosen by date. Threading also affects the display.

■ In the Options menu, choose Add from Newest Messages if you want to load in messages starting with the most recently posted ones. Choose Add from Oldest Messages if you want to load in messages starting from the oldest ones.

Figure 12.46 *Select the desired newsgroup (or any message it contains).*

Figure 12.47 *Choose Get More Messages in the File menu.*

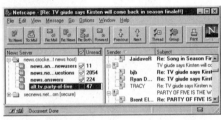

Figure 12.48 *More messages are displayed in the right pane.*

Figure 12.49 *At the bottom of the Server preferences tab, type a number next to Get xx Messages at a time (Max 3500).*

Getting more messages

Reading and Posting News

Figure 13.1 *Click the newsgroup's name in the left pane of the News window.*

Figure 13.2 *Click a message in the right pane to display its contents in the lower pane.*

Figure 13.3 *When you're reading messages, make the right pane wider so that you can see the title of each message more clearly.*

The main difference between working with newsgroups and using e-mail is that newsgroup postings disappear, while mail remains on your hard disk.

Reading the postings in a newsgroup

You don't have to subscribe to a newsgroup *(see page 149)* in order to read or reply to the postings that it contains.

To read a newsgroup's postings:

1. Click the newsgroup in the left pane of the News window **(Fig. 13.1)**. The postings are shown in the right pane of the News window.

2. Click a posting in the right pane to display its contents in the lower pane of the News window **(Figure 13.2)**.

3. Use the scroll bars to view more of the message as necessary.

4. Navigate to read more messages *(see page 114)*.

✔ Tips

■ Adjust the width of the panes to suit the task at hand **(Figure 13.3)**. For more information, see *Changing the size of the panes* on page 106.

■ You can show additional information about a message, including the route it took to get to you (which is sometimes useful for exposing fraudulent messages), by choosing All under Show Headers in the Options menu.

Posting a message to a newsgroup

With e-mail, you can only send messages to people you already know, or at least have the address of. In a newsgroup, you can post a message that may be seen by thousands of people you've never met. The one restriction about posting messages to a newsgroup is the topic. You should restrict your subject matter to that which is usually discussed in that newsgroup. Check the FAQ if you're not sure *(see page 143)*.

To post a message to a newsgroup:

1. In the News window, select the newsgroup—or a message in that group—where you want to post a message **(Figure 13.4)**.

2. Choose New News Message in the File menu or click the To: News button **(Figure 13.5)**. A fresh Message Composition window appears. The selected newsgroup is automatically filled in in the Newsgroups field **(Figure 13.6)**.

3. Type the subject of the message in the Subject field **(Figure 13.7)**. The subject is important: as the most visible part of the message, it can mean the difference between people reading your message or ignoring it.

4. Type the contents of the message in the area at the bottom of the window.

5. Choose Send Now (or Send Later) in the File menu or click the Send button to send the message **(Figure 13.8)**.

Figure 13.4 *In the News window, select the newsgroup—or a posting in that group—to which you wish to post a message.*

Figure 13.5 *Choose New News Message in the File menu (left) or click the To: News button on the toolbar (right).*

Figure 13.6 *The Message Composition window appears with the name of the newsgroup automatically entered in the Newsgroups field.*

Figure 13.7 *Type the subject in the Subject field and the contents of the posting in the lower area.*

Posting a message to a newsgroup

Figure 13.8 *Choose Send Now (or Send Later) in the File menu.*

Figure 13.9 *If the Newsgroups field does not appear, you probably didn't choose a newsgroup before choosing To: News.*

Figure 13.10 *Simply choose Newsgroups in the View menu to make the Newsgroups field appear in the Message Composition window.*

Figure 13.11 *The Newsgroups field appears. Now you can type the name of the newsgroup and post the message.*

✔ **Tips**

■ Posting a message is virtually the same as sending e-mail. The only difference is that an e-mail message requires use of the Mail To field, while a news posting uses the Newsgroups field.

■ Click the Address button (or any of the Mail To, Cc, etc. buttons) to make the Address Book appear.

■ By default, your messages are posted immediately—although it may take a little while before they appear in the newsgroup. For information on deferred posting, consult *Composing postings offline* on page 159.

■ If the Newsgroups field doesn't appear, you probably didn't select the newsgroup before opening the Message Composition window **(Figure 13.9)**. Choose Newsgroups in the View menu **(Figure 13.10)** to make the field appear **(Figure 13.11)** and type in the newsgroup's name. For more information on message parts, consult *Viewing or hiding the parts of a message* on page 116.

■ You can post a message to several newsgroups at once. Separate each newsgroup name with a comma.

■ You attach a URL or file to a news message in exactly the same way as you attach one to an e-mail message. For more information, consult *Attaching files to a message* on page 126 or *Attaching a URL to a message* on page 127.

■ Keep the Wrap Long Lines command in the View menu active to ensure that outgoing messages have the returns between lines.

Posting a message to a newsgroup

Replying to a newsgroup post

There are three ways to respond to a message in a newsgroup. If you want everyone in the newsgroup to see your reply, post the response to the newsgroup. If you only want the original sender to receive the reply, e-mail him or her directly. Finally, you can simultaneously post and mail a message to cover all your bases.

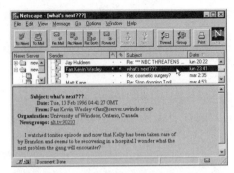

Figure 13.12 *Select the posting that you want to reply to in the right pane of the News window.*

To reply to a newsgroup post:

1. Select the message that you wish to reply to in the upper right pane of the News window **(Figure 13.12)**.

2. In the Message menu, choose Post Reply to have your reply appear in the newsgroup **(Fig. 13.13)**. Choose Mail Reply to e-mail your reply only to the writer of the original message **(Fig. 13.14)**. Choose Post and Mail Reply to do both things **(Fig. 13.15)**.

3. The Message Composition window appears, with the appropriate fields automatically filled in. The Newsgroups field only appears in postings, the Mail To field only appears in mail.

4. Choose Send Now (or Send Later) in the File menu.

Figure 13.13 *Choose Post Reply in the Message menu (left) to publish the posting in the newsgroup. Notice that the Newsgroups field appears but the Mail To field does not (right).*

Figure 13.14 *Choose Mail Reply in the Message menu (left) to mail the posting to the original sender. Notice that the Mail To field appears but the Newsgroups field does not (right).*

✔ Tips

■ Generally, you are supposed to try and limit your postings to information that will interest the entire newsgroup. Mail a response when it applies only to the particular recipient.

■ Sometimes, people post messages and then don't check to see if they have any responses. You can post *and* mail a message to make sure that both the newsgroup members and the recipient receive (and see) a copy.

Figure 13.15 *Choose Post and Mail Reply in the Message menu (left) to publish the posting in the newsgroup and send a copy to the original sender. Notice that both the Newsgroups and Mail To fields appear (right).*

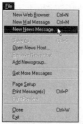

Figure 13.16
Choose New News Message in the File menu (left) or click the To: News button on the toolbar (right).

Figure 13.17 *Type the message in the Message Composition window.*

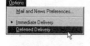

Figure 13.18 *Choose Deferred Delivery in the Options menu.*

Figure 13.19
Choose Send Later in the File menu (left) or click the Send button (right) on the toolbar.

Figure 13.20 *Go to the Mail window and click the Outbox to see the outgoing posting.*

Composing postings offline

When you receive an e-mail message, Netscape downloads it to your hard disk, making it easy to reply to later, even if you're not connected to your Internet account. However, when you read a news posting, the message is not downloaded to your hard disk. So even though you can compose a new posting or a reply offline, you can't browse the existing messages and respond to them directly.

To compose postings offline:

1. Disconnect from the Internet without quitting Netscape (or launch Netscape without connecting to the Internet).

2. Choose New News Message in the File menu **(Figure 13.16)**. The Message Composition window appears.

3. Compose the posting as usual *(see pages 156 and 158)* **(Figure 13.17)**. If you are replying to a posting, type **Re: subject** in the Subject field where *subject* is the original topic.

4. In the Message Composition window's Options menu, choose Deferred Delivery **(Figure 13.18)**.

5. Choose Send Later in the File menu or click the Send button on the toolbar **(Fig. 13.19)**. The message is stored in the Outbox in the Mail window **(Figure 13.20)**.

6. When you're ready to send the posting(s), consult *Sending the messages in the Outbox* on page 119.

✔ Tip

■ Leave the newsgroup open before disconnecting and make the window as large as possible, so that you can at least see all the postings' subject lines.

Composing postings offline

Sending mail from the News window

Reading a posting in the News window may motivate you to write someone. Perhaps it will just spark your imagination, perhaps you'll want to tell her about something you've read or offer a link to a newsgroup. At any rate, the process is virtually identical to sending e-mail from the Mail window.

To send mail from the News window:

1. Choose New Mail Message in the File menu or click To: Mail on the toolbar **(Fig. 13.21)**. The Message Composition window appears **(Figure 13.22)**.

2. Compose the message as usual *(see page 115)*.

3. If desired, add a link to the newsgroup that inspired you by typing **news:name.newsgroup** in the message area where *name.newsgroup* is the complete name of the newsgroup **(Figure 13.23)**. If the recipient reads the message with Netscape 2 or 3, the newsgroup will appear as a link, and a click on it will open the newsgroup for him or her **(Figure 13.24)**.

Figure 13.21 *From the News window itself, choose New Mail Message in the File menu.*

Figure 13.22 *An empty Message Composition window appears.*

Figure 13.23 *Compose your messages as usual.*

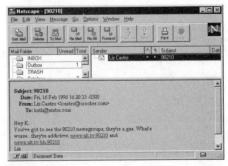

Figure 13.24 *Go to the Mail window and click the Outbox to see the outgoing message.*

Sending mail from the News window

Part II:
Netscape Navigator Gold

Creating your own Web pages

The Editor Window

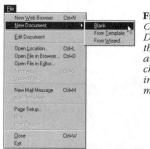

Figure 14.1 *Choose New Document in the File menu and then choose Blank in the submenu.*

The Editor window is where you create new Web pages and modify existing ones. The Editor window has three unique toolbars and some special menu commands.

There are several ways to open the Editor window, depending on whether you wish to start a new page or modify existing ones.

Opening a blank Editor window

Figure 14.2 *An empty Editor window appears.*

If you wish to start a Web page completely from scratch, you should open a blank Editor window. Then you will be able to create a page using the instructions in this and subsequent chapters.

To open a blank Editor window:

1. Make sure you are in a browser, and not in the News or Mail windows.

2. Choose New Document in the File menu and Blank in the submenu that appears **(Figure 14.1)**. An empty Editor window appears **(Fig. 14.2)**.

Figure 14.3 *Or, with a blank page in the browser showing, click the Edit button on the toolbar.*

✔ Tips

■ You can also open a blank page by clicking the New Document button 🗒 on the toolbar and choosing Blank Document in the dialog that appears.

■ If you have specified a blank page as your home page *(see page 17)*, you can open a blank Editor window by clicking the Edit icon on the browser window's toolbar **(Figure 14.3)**.

■ Close the Editor window by choosing Close in the File menu.

Opening a new page with a template

Netscape Communications has developed a set of templates that you can use as a starting off point for your Web pages. There are templates for home pages and for small businesses, for resumes and job listings, for special interest groups and for special interest people.

Each template contains sample images, text and links that you should replace with your own elements. Note that the links on the pages don't go anywhere; they're just designed to give you ideas.

To open a new page with a template:

1. Open your Internet connection.

2. From either the Editor window or the browser, choose New Document in the File menu and then choose From Template in the submenu **(Fig. 14.4)**. A browser will appear with the current collection of Netscape's templates **(Figure 14.5)**.

3. Navigate to the desired template and click its link. The template appears in the browser **(Figure 14.6)**.

4. Choose Edit Document in the File menu or click the Edit button on the toolbar. Since you must save a document before modifying it, the Save Remote Document dialog box appears **(Figure 14.7)**.

5. Check the Adjust links to assist in remote publishing option so that Netscape adapts the links in the page that you are browsing so that it works in a local setting (and you can test it).

Figure 14.4
Choose New Document in the File menu and then choose From Template in the submenu.

Figure 14.5 *Click the desired template's link.*

Figure 14.6 *The template appears in the browser. A template may include images, text and links that you can replace with your own.*

Figure 14.7 *The Save Remote Document appears whenever you try to edit a page from the Web that you have not yet saved. Generally, you should check both options and click Save.*

Figure 14.8 *You are not allowed to copy any images you find out on the Web for your page. Click OK.*

Figure 14.9 *Enter a name for the page and choose a location on your hard disk. Then click Save.*

Figure 14.10 *The template is opened in the Editor window. Change the text, images and links to suit your needs.*

6. Check the Save images with document option. If you don't, Netscape only saves the text, that is, the HTML tags that make up the document.

7. Click Save.

8. A dialog box may appear warning you about copyright issues **(Figure 14.8)**. You may not copy any images you find on the Web without permission. Click OK.

9. In the standard Save dialog box that appears **(Figure 14.9)**, choose a name and location for the page and click Save. The template will appear in the Editor window **(Fig. 14.10)**.

10. Modify the template to suit your needs, replacing the generic elements on the template with the components of your real page.

11. Choose Save in the File menu to save the changes periodically.

✔ Tips

- You can also open a new page with a template by clicking the New Document button 🗋 on the File/Edit Tools toolbar and then clicking From Template in the dialog box that appears.

- You must be connected to the Internet to be able to access Netscape's templates.

- You can create your own templates and then set up Netscape to open *them* when you choose New Document/From Template in the File menu *(see page 254)*.

Opening a new page with a template

Opening a new page with the Page Wizard

Netscape has also set up a special script that takes information entered into a form and converts it into a Web page. You can then use the generated Web page as is or modify it further as desired.

To open a new page with the Page Wizard:

1. Open your Internet connection.

2. From the browser or Editor window, choose New Document from the File menu and then From Wizard in the submenu **(Figure 14.11)**. Netscape's Page Wizard is displayed.

3. In the upper right frame, read the text and then scroll down to the bottom and click Start **(Figure 14.12)**. The introduction and page creation guide appear in the left frame.

4. Under content, click the "give your page a title" link. The bottom frame displays a text box in which you can type your page's title **(Figure 14.13)**.

5. Enter a title in the bottom frame and click Apply. The new title is previewed in the right frame.

6. Scroll down to the next section in the left frame. Continue using the links in the left frame and the corresponding options in the bottom frame to design your page. When you're finished, click Build. The completed page is displayed in the browser **(Figure 14.14)**.

7. Choose Edit Document in the File menu or click the Edit button to view the new page in the Editor window **(Figure 14.15)**.

Figure 14.11 *Choose New Document in the File menu and then choose From Wizard in the submenu.*

Figure 14.12 *Netscape's Page Wizard is a set of frames. Scroll down in the first frame (showing) and click Start to begin your page.*

Figure 14.13 *The left frame guides you through the page creation process. When you click on a step, the lower frame offers options from which to choose, or a text box in which you can enter information. The right frame displays a preview of your page.*

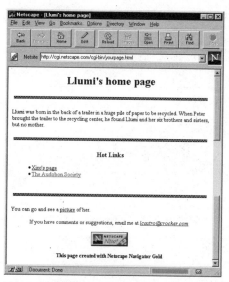

Figure 14.14 *Your page is generated from the responses given on the form. Notice the Netscape Gold logo at the bottom of the page.*

Figure 14.15 *Choose Edit Document in the File menu (or click the Edit button on the toolbar).*

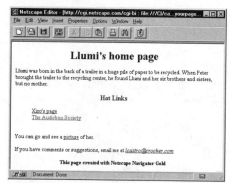

Figure 14.16 *You can polish the generated page in the Editor window.*

8. The Save Remote Document will appear. Make sure both options are checked and click Save.

9. The Copyright warning dialog box may appear. Read it and click OK. The images in the generated page are not copyrighted.

10. In the Save dialog box that appears, give the page file a name and choose a location for it. Then click OK. The generated page appears in the Editor window **(Figure 14.16)**.

11. Edit the page as desired.

12. Choose Save in the File menu to save the changes periodically.

✔ Tips

■ You can also jump to Netscape's Page Wizard by clicking the New Document button on the File/Edit Tools toolbar and then clicking From Page Wizard in the dialog box that appears.

■ Be careful to choose a background pattern that contrasts enough with the text color so that people can read your page.

■ If you don't like the way the page comes out, click the Back button, change the desired options (everything will be just as you left it) and click Create Page again.

■ Netscape inserts its own logo at the bottom of every page created with the Page Wizard. If you don't feel like doing your part to advertise Netscape's stock, just erase it once you're in the Editor window.

■ You have to be connected to the Internet to use the Page Wizard.

Editing an existing page

You may save Web pages that you find on the Web and edit them to create new pages. This is a good way to learn different Web page construction techniques, although you should keep in mind that the images and text you find may be copyrighted, and at any rate, should not be used in your Web page without permission.

To edit an existing page:

1. Navigate to the page that you wish to edit **(Figure 14.17)**.

2. Choose Edit Document in the File menu or click the Edit button on the toolbar. The Save Remote Document dialog box appears **(Figure 14.18)**.

3. Check both options in the Save Remote Document dialog box and click Save.

4. The copyright warning dialog box appears. Read it and click OK.

5. In the Save As dialog box that appears, enter a name and choose a location for the file and then click Save **(Figure 14.19)**. The page is displayed in the Editor window **(Figure 14.20)**.

✔ Tip

■ You shouldn't copy any text or images from another page without permission. Besides being against the law, it's pretty slimy. Instead, use other pages as a source of inspiration. Then write your own text and draw or scan your own pictures.

Figure 14.17 *Navigate to the desired page and click the Edit button on the toolbar.*

Figure 14.18 *You should generally check both options in the Save Remote Document dialog box.*

Figure 14.19 *Enter a name and choose a location for the file and then click Save.*

Figure 14.20 *The page viewed in the Editor window.*

Figure 14.21 *If you have the Editor window active, choose Open File in the File menu (left). If a browser is active, the option will be Open File in Editor (right).*

Figure 14.22 *Find the file on your hard disk that you wish to edit. You can open any text file, as long as it has the .htm or .html extension.*

Figure 14.23 *Once the text file is in the Editor window, you can format it and add images and links.*

Editing a saved file

You don't have to go out on the Web to find a page to copy. You can open any HTML file that you have previously created or saved—indeed *any* text file—in the Editor window.

To edit a saved file:

1. Make sure the saved file is either an HTML or text only document. In both cases, it must carry either the .htm or .html extension.

2. If you're in the Editor window, choose Open File in the File menu. With a browser active, choose Open File in Editor in the File menu **(Fig. 14.21)**. The Open dialog box appears.

3. Navigate to the desired file and click Open **(Fig. 14.22)**. The file appears in the Editor window **(Figure 14.23)**.

✔ Tips

■ If you want to convert an existing document into a Web page, first save it in Text only format with the .htm extension. Then open it in the Editor window.

■ You are not limited to documents created with Netscape. Any text document will do.

Editing a saved file

Adding a title and keywords

The title and keywords of a page, and in lesser degree, the author, description, and classification, are used by search services to categorize Web pages. By creating a descriptive title and inserting specific keywords, you make it easier for people to find your page.

To add a title and keywords:

1. With the Editor window active, choose Document in the Properties menu **(Figure 14.24)**. The Document Properties dialog box appears.

2. Enter a title for your page **(Fig. 14.25)**. Make it short (less than 60 characters) and descriptive.

3. If desired, enter your name in the Author field, and a short description in the Description field.

4. In the Keywords field, type three or four important words that appear on your page or that your page is about.

5. If desired, type a category in the Classification field.

6. Click OK to save the changes. The new title appears in the title bar, in front of the page's file name **(Figure 14.26)**.

✔ Tip

■ You can set the Author name in the Editor Preferences dialog box *(see page 254)* so that you don't have to type it in each time.

Figure 14.24 *Choose Document in the Properties menu.*

Figure 14.25 *In the Document Properties dialog box, fill in the fields and then click OK.*

Figure 14.26 *The new title appears in the title bar, in front of the page's file name.*

Adding a title and keywords

Figure 14.27 *Choose Save in the File menu.*

Figure 14.28 *Give the file a name, choose a location, make sure the format is HTML Files, and then click Save.*

Figure 14.29 *The new file name appears in the title bar.*

Saving your Web page

It's important to save your Web pages frequently while creating them.

To save your Web page:

1. With the Editor window active, choose Save in the File menu **(Figure 14.27)**.

2. If you have not saved the file before, the Save As dialog box will appear. Enter a name and location for the document and make sure that HTML Files appears in the Save File as Type pop-up menu **(Figure 14.28)**.

3. Click Save. The document is saved and the new file name appears in the title bar **(Figure 14.29)**.

✔ Tips

■ You can set Netscape up to save your file automatically every few minutes. For more information, see page 254.

■ After you've saved the document once, choose Save to save additional changes and Save As to save the document with a new name or location.

■ You can also save a Web page by clicking the Save Document button 🖫 on the File/Edit Tools toolbar.

■ The first time you create a link or insert an image on a page, Netscape will automatically make you save the page on your hard disk.

■ If you try and close a page without saving the changes, Netscape will give you a chance to save the page.

The Editor window's toolbars

The Editor window has three toolbars:
File/Edit Tools **(Figure 14.30)**, Paragraph
Properties **(Figure 14.31)**, and Character
Properties **(Figure 14.32)**. The buttons
on the toolbars are simply shortcuts to
menu commands.

Figure 14.30 *The File/Edit Tools toolbar
contains many of the commands available in
the File and Edit menus.*

Figure 14.31 *The Paragraph Properties contains
formatting commands that affect the entire paragraph (not just a few words).*

Figure 14.32 *The Character Properties toolbar
contains formatting commands that affect
individual characters or words, as well as the
Insert commands.*

Figure 14.33 *Each time you open a new Editor window, the three toolbars appear aligned to the left at the top of the window in individual rows.*

Figure 14.34 *You can drag any toolbar to any other row, or even to the bottom of the window, as shown here.*

Figure 14.35 *You can also drag the toolbars horizontally.*

Figure 14.36 *If you drag the toolbar outside of the toolbar areas (top or bottom) it becomes a floating palette.*

Repositioning the toolbars

The Editor window's toolbars are very flexible. You can move them around the toolbar area, drag them out of the toolbar area altogether, or hide them completely.

To move a toolbar:

Drag the toolbar from the current row to the desired location in the top or bottom toolbar area **(Figure 14.34)**. You can also shift toolbars horizontally **(Figure 14.35)**.

To convert a toolbar into a floating palette:

Drag the desired toolbar outside the toolbar area. The toolbar changes into a floating palette and acquires a close box **(Figure 14.36)**. Drag it back to the top or bottom toolbar area to convert it back into a fixed toolbar.

To hide or show the toolbars:

In the Options menu, choose Show File/ Edit Toolbar, Show Character Format Toolbar, or Show Paragraph Format Toolbar. When a checkmark appears, the toolbar is visible. Choose the command again to toggle it.

✔ Tips

■ The configuration of one Editor window's toolbars does not affect the other Editor windows' toolbars.

■ You can tell if a toolbar is going to be turned into a palette by the size of the shadow as you drag it. A smaller shadow means it will stay a toolbar. A larger shadow means it will be a palette.

Repositioning the toolbars

173

Viewing tables and paragraph marks

Netscape 3 offers two miscellaneous viewing options in the Editor window that make work a bit easier and faster. First, you can view tables without formatting, saving time and memory. Second, you can choose to view paragraph marks, in order to more easily determine where you are and where you wish to make changes.

To view tables without formatting:

Choose Display Tables in the View menu **(Figure 14.38)**. When the option has a checkmark, tables are viewed normally. When the option has no checkmark, tables are viewed without formatting **(Figure 14.39)**.

To view paragraph marks:

Choose Display Paragraph Marks in the View menu **(Figure 14.40)**. When the option has a checkmark, you'll be able to see small rectangles at the end of each paragraph **(Figure 14.41)**. When the option is not checked, the paragraph marks will be invisible.

Figure 14.37 *Viewing tables can be slow and memory intensive.*

Figure 14.38 *Choose Display Tables to remove the checkmark from the option.*

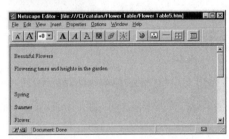

Figure 14.39 *The table is viewed as a list.*

Figure 14.40 *Choose Display Paragraph Marks in the View menu to show the division between paragraphs.*

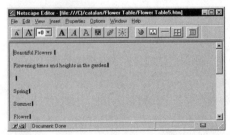

Figure 14.41 *The small black rectangles indicate the carriage returns, and thus, distinct paragraphs.*

Formatting a Web Page

Figure 15.1 *Select the text or graphic element that you wish to adjust. Here I've selected a graphic image.*

Figure 15.2 *Click the Object Properties button on the Character Properties toolbar.*

Figure 15.3 *Depending on what you had selected, the appropriate dialog box appears. Make any necessary changes and click OK.*

A Web page is not just a regular word processing document. Its formatting is added with special tags that enable you to save the page in text only format. This means that the document can be read by almost any computer. Although you could write the tags, called HTML, with any word processor—even WordPad—the Editor window in Netscape Gold has one important advantage: instead of showing the tags, it shows you the actual formatting.

HTML was designed to be a universal language, equally intelligible from a PC as from a Mac, or even a UNIX computer. For that reason, not all formats are available in the Editor window. For example, you can't choose a font for the page. Although this might be frustrating for font aficionados, it's a blessing for the rest of us who may have a more limited supply.

The Object Properties button

Throughout this chapter we talk about the individual methods you have for formatting a Web page. The Object Properties button, on the Character Properties toolbar, automatically opens the appropriate dialog box depending on what you have selected. You can use it to adjust the formatting of *any* element on your Web page.

To use the Object Properties button:

Select the element or text that you wish to modify **(Figure 15.1)** and click the Object Properties button **(Figure 15.2)**. The appropriate dialog box will appear **(Figure 15.3)**. Continue as usual.

Adding basic character formatting

As in word processors and page layout software, character formatting means any style that can be added to a single character or word. *Basic* character formatting means bold, italic, underlined, fixed width, strikethrough, superscript, subscript, and blinking **(Figure 15.4)**.

To add basic character formatting:

1. Select the character(s) you wish to modify **(Figure 15.5)**.

2. Choose Character in the Properties menu and then choose the desired style in the submenu **(Figure 15.6)**. The changes are applied to the text immediately **(Figure 15.7)**.

✔ Tips

■ If you don't select anything before applying styles, the formatting will be applied to the next thing you type.

■ You can also apply character formatting by checking an option in the Style section of the Character Properties dialog box *(see page 179)*.

■ Apply bold, italic and fixed width formatting by clicking the corresponding button on the Character Properties toolbar: **A**, *A* or A, respectively.

■ Unfortunately, Netscape Gold only uses *physical* formatting like bold and italic. To apply *logical* formatting like emphasis or strong, you must add the HTML tag manually. For more information, consult *Adding HTML tags manually* on page 230.

Figure 15.4 *All character styles except* Blink *are displayed properly in the Editor window. To see blinking text, you have to view the file in a browser.*

Figure 15.5 *Select the letters or words that you wish to format.*

Figure 15.6 *Choose Character in the Properties menu and then choose the desired style in the submenu.*

Figure 15.7 *The selected word now appears in bold formatting.*

Figure 15.8 *There are seven possible sizes, two smaller than the base size and four larger.*

Figure 15.9 *Select the letter that you want to change. Here, only the initial O is selected.*

Figure 15.10 *Choose the desired size in the Font Size submenu in the Properties menu.*

Figure 15.11 *The initial O is now several sizes larger than the rest of the text.*

Figure 15.12 *You can also apply a new size by choosing it from the Font Size pop-up menu on the Paragraph Properties toolbar.*

Changing the size of text

You may change the size of certain words to give them emphasis **(Figure 15.8)**. Unfortunately, the font size is not a standard HTML tag and may not be recognized by other Web browsers besides Netscape. For more information, consult *Standard HTML* on page 228.

To change the size of text:

1. Select the character(s) that you wish to make larger or smaller **(Fig. 15.9)**.

2. Choose Font Size in the Properties menu and then a relative size in the submenu that appears **(Fig. 15.10)**. The text is changed **(Figure 15.11)**.

✔ Tips

■ You can't choose an absolute size for text; each paragraph has a size, and you can modify individual characters with respect to that size. In addition, the sizes you choose all depend on the font that your reader has chosen to view your page with *(see page 20)*.

■ You can also click the Decrease Font Size icon A in the Character Properties toolbar to make text one unit smaller. Click the Increase Font Size icon A to make text one unit larger.

■ Use the Font Size pop-up menu to choose a particular (relative) size **(Figure 15.12)**.

■ As illustrated in the example, changing the size of an individual letter may change the spacing (leading) of the entire line. There's no simple solution. (The hard solution is to insert an *image* of the opening letter and wrap the text around it—see page 194.)

Changing the color of text

You should be a little careful about changing the color of the text on your Web page. First of all, some colors already have standard uses, like blue for links and purple for visited links. Secondly, the colors should have good contrast with the background color or image. Finally, realize that not all of your readers will have color screens (or they may choose to view pages with their own colors) and may not benefit from your efforts.

To change the color of text:

1. Select the character(s) that you wish to change the color of **(Figure 15.13)**.

2. Choose Character in the Properties menu and then Text Color in the submenu that appears **(Figure 15.14)**. The Color dialog box appears.

3. Click the desired color for the text and click OK **(Figure 15.15)**. The text changes color **(Figure 15.16)**.

✔ Tips

■ You can also change the color of text by clicking the Font Color button 🔳 on the Character Properties toolbar.

■ Change text back to its default color by selecting the text and choosing Default Color in the Character submenu under Properties. The default colors are specified in the Document Properties dialog box. Typically, regular text is black, links are blue, visited links are purple and active links are red.

Figure 15.13 *Select the letters or words that you wish to change.*

Figure 15.14 *Choose Character in the Properties menu and then Text Color in the submenu.*

Figure 15.15 *Click the desired color in the Color dialog box and then click OK.*

Figure 15.16 *The text is changed to the selected color.*

Figure 15.17 *Select the text you wish to change.*

Figure 15.18 *Choose Text in the Properties menu.*

Figure 15.19 *Choose the desired character styles in the Character Properties dialog box and then click Apply or OK.*

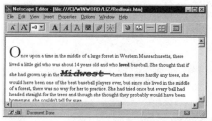

Figure 15.20 *All the chosen styles are applied to the selected text.*

Applying many character styles at once

Although there are about twelve ways to apply character formatting (OK, maybe four), one of the nicest is through the Character Properties dialog box, since you can apply several styles at once, see the changes without closing the dialog box, modify the options, and try again and again until you're satisfied with the results.

To apply many character styles at once:

1. Select the character(s) that you wish to modify **(Figure 15.17)**.

2. Choose Text in the Properties menu **(Figure 15.18)**. The Properties dialog box appears.

3. Click the Character tab to see the Character properties.

4. Check the desired character styles, select a size and choose a color for the text **(Figure 15.19)**.

5. If desired, click Apply to apply the changes without closing the dialog box. You may then check or uncheck the desired options, and click Apply again until you are satisfied.

6. Click OK (or Close if you've already applied the changes) to close the Character Properties dialog box. All the changes are applied **(Fig. 15.20)**.

✔ Tip

■ You can make the Character Properties box appear by right clicking the text selection and selecting Character properties in the pop-up menu that appears.

Clearing character styles

Sometimes it's easy to go overboard with character formatting. Luckily, it's easy to get rid of. Netscape has two commands for clearing character styles. One eliminates only the basic character styles like bold and italic while the other eliminates all possible character styling, including size, color, and JavaScript coding.

To clear character styles:

1. Select the desired text and choose Text in the Properties menu **(Figure 15.21)**.

2. Click the Character tab to see the Character properties.

3. To eliminate basic style settings click Clear Style Settings. To eliminate all character formatting, click Clear All Settings **(Figure 15.22)**.

4. Click Apply to apply the changes without closing the dialog box.

5. Click OK (or Close if you've already applied the changes) to close the dialog box. The formatting is removed **(Figure 15.23)**.

✔ Tips

■ Another way to "deformat" text is by clicking the Clear All Styles button on the Character Properties toolbar or selecting Clear all character styles in the Properties menu under Character **(Figure 15.24)**.

■ You can open the Character Properties box by right clicking the text and choosing Character Properties in the submenu that appears.

Figure 15.21 *Choose Text in the Properties menu.*

Figure 15.22 *Click Clear Style Settings (left with the arrow) to remove all the basic character styles. Click Clear All Settings to reset all the styles in this dialog box to their defaults. Then click Apply or OK.*

Figure 15.23 *All of the formatting is removed from the selected text.*

Figure 15.24 *Another way to remove all of the character formatting is by choosing Character in the Properties menu and then Clear all character styles in the submenu.*

Clearing character styles

Figure 15.25 *In this page,* Red and Louis *is formatted with Heading 1,* Introduction *and* Chapter 1 *are formatted with Heading 2. The rest of the text is Normal.*

Figure 15.26 *Here we have an unordered list, with round bullets, and a table made from formatted text (that is, fixed width text). At the bottom of the page is the author's name, formatted with Address.*

Using paragraph styles

Paragraph styles, by definition, affect an entire paragraph. In Netscape Gold, and indeed in HTML in general, the styles are already defined and each browser on each platform interprets them in its own way. This way, you can distinguish one paragraph from another and organize your information without restricting your page to a particular platform.

To use paragraph styles:

1. Decide how you want to organize your information. Divide your page into sections, with descriptive headings. Apply the Heading styles to section heads **(Figure 15.25)**.

2. Use the List Item for lists. There are several kinds: Numbered, Unnumbered (unordered), Directory, Menu, and Description **(Fig. 15.26)**. Lists are described more fully on page 183.

3. The Formatted style (known as *Preformatted* in regular HTML lingo) is for fixed width text like handmade tables **(Figure 15.26)** or ASCII images. All spaces are maintained and the text is displayed in a fixed width font like Courier.

4. Use the Address style to format your name and e-mail address as a signature at the bottom of the page **(Figure 15.26)**.

5. Use Description Title and Description Text to format the pairs of entries in Description lists.

Using paragraph styles

Applying paragraph styles

Once you've figured out which paragraph styles to use, applying them is quite easy.

To apply paragraph styles:

1. Click anywhere in the paragraph that you wish to modify **(Figure 15.27)**. You don't need to select the whole paragraph.

2. Select Paragraph in the Properties menu and then choose the desired paragraph style in the submenu that appears **(Figure 15.28)**. The entire paragraph is affected **(Figure 15.29)**.

✔ Tips

■ You can also apply paragraph styles by choosing the desired option in the Paragraph style pop-up menu on the Paragraph Properties toolbar **(Figure 15.30)**.

■ One more way to apply paragraph styles is with the Paragraph Properties dialog box *(see page 188)*—which you can open by right clicking the desired paragraph and choosing Paragraph/List properties in the submenu that appears.

Figure 15.27 *Click in the paragraph you want to format.*

Figure 15.28 *Choose Paragraph in the Properties menu and then choose the desired style in the submenu.*

Figure 15.29 *The whole paragraph is formatted.*

Figure 15.30 *You can also choose styles in the Style pop-up menu on the Paragraph Properties toolbar.*

Applying paragraph styles

Figure 15.31 *Click in the paragraph where you want to create a list. You needn't type anything.*

Figure 15.32 *Choose Paragraph in the Properties menu. Then choose List Item in the submenu.*

Figure 15.33 *You can tell by the bullet that the paragraph is formatted as a list.*

Figure 15.34 *Choose Text in the Properties menu.*

Creating lists

While applying other paragraph styles is a one step process as described on page 182, creating a list has two parts: applying a list style and choosing what kind of list you want it to be.

To create a list:

1. Place the cursor in the paragraph that you want to convert into a list item **(Figure 15.31)**. There doesn't have to be text in it yet.

2. Select Paragraph in the Properties menu and then choose List Item in the submenu that appears **(Fig. 15.32)**. The selected paragraph is converted into a list item in an unnumbered list (*unordered*, in HTML lingo) and the bullet of the first line appears **(Figure 15.33)**.

3. If you want to choose a different kind of list, select Text in the Properties menu **(Figure 15.34)**. The Properties dialog box appears.

4. Click the Paragraph tab to see the Paragraph Properties. The Paragraph style will already show List Item. Choose List in the Additional style pop-up menu if it's not already selected.

5. In the List section, which is now active, choose the kind of list you want to create **(Figure 15.35)**.

6. For unnumbered lists, you can select what kinds of bullets should be used in the Bullet Style pop-up menu. If you've chosen the Numbered list style, you can decide what kind of numbering to use with the Number Style pop-up menu. Then choose an initial number for the list in the Starting number text box.

7. If desired, click Apply to apply the changes without closing the dialog box. Make additional changes and apply them until you are satisfied.

8. Click OK (or Close if you've previously applied the changes) to close the dialog box. The changes will be evident **(Figure 15.36)**.

9. Type the contents of the list if you haven't done so already, adding a return after each list item **(Fig. 15.37)**.

✔ Tips

■ Use the Bullet List button or the Numbered List button on the Paragraph Properties toolbar to change a list from one format to the other.

■ If you have any characters selected in a list item line before using the unnumbered or numbered list buttons on the toolbar, the changes affect the selected line and the one preceding it. With the cursor in the list item but with nothing selected, the changes affect all the lines in the list, both above and below the current one.

■ After you're finished typing a list and you choose Normal style to add some more body text, Netscape doesn't quite make the paragraph normal, but instead makes it *indented* normal. To make it really normal, click the Remove one indent level button on the Paragraph Properties toolbar.

■ The numbers in a numbered list do not appear until you browse the page **(Figure 15.38)**. Until then, they are shown as ##. All initial letters appear as lowercase *a*.

Figure 15.35 *Choose List in Additional Style and select the type of list in the Style menu. Then choose a bullet or number style. Finally, click OK.*

Figure 15.36 *In the Editor window, Numbered lists with letters are shown with a lower case a.*

Figure 15.37 *Type the list, placing a return after each item. You could just as easily type the list at the beginning and then format it using the same steps.*

Figure 15.38 *When you view the page with a browser, the letters appear as they should: capital, sequential, starting with C (see Figure 15.35) and with a period after each initial letter.*

Creating lists

Figure 15.39 *Click anywhere in the paragraph that you want to indent.*

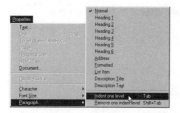

Figure 15.40 *Choose Paragraph in the Properties menu and then Indent one level in the submenu.*

Figure 15.41 *The entire paragraph is indented.*

Indenting a paragraph

HTML does not accept multiple spaces or returns. If you try and type two spaces, the program will simply ignore you. However, Netscape Gold lets you indent an entire paragraph, with a device that approximates a tab.

To indent a paragraph:

1. Place the cursor anywhere in the paragraph that you want to indent **(Figure 15.39)**. You don't have to select anything.

2. Choose Paragraph in the Properties menu and choose Indent one level in the submenu **(Figure 15.40)**. The paragraph is indented toward the right **(Figure 15.41)**.

When you remove an indent from a paragraph, the whole paragraph is shifted back toward the left.

To remove an indent:

1. Place the cursor anywhere in an indented paragraph.

2. Choose Paragraph in the Properties menu and then choose Remove one indent level in the submenu that appears. The indent disappears and the paragraph is moved to the left.

✔ Tips

■ You can also add an indent with the Tab key and remove one using Shift+Tab. It's strange, but it even works in the middle or end of a line.

■ Or use the Increase Indent button 🔳 or the Decrease Indent button 🔳 on the Paragraph Properties toolbar.

Indenting a paragraph

Aligning text

You can align the text on your page to the left or to the right, or you can center it. By default, all paragraphs are aligned to the left.

To align text:

1. Click anywhere in the paragraph you wish to align **(Figure 15.42)**. You don't have to select anything.

2. Choose Text in the Properties menu. The Properties dialog box appears.

3. Click the Paragraph tab to see the Paragraph Properties.

4. Click the desired alignment option at the bottom of the dialog box **(Figure 15.43)**.

5. If desired, click Apply to apply the changes without closing the dialog box. Change the options and click Apply again until you are satisfied with the results.

6. Click OK (or Close if you've applied the changes) to close the dialog box. The text is aligned as specified **(Figure 15.44)**.

✔ Tip

■ You can also align text by choosing the Align Left 🖪, Center 🖫 or Align Right 🖫 buttons on the Paragraph Properties toolbar.

Figure 15.42 *Click anywhere in the paragraph whose alignment you want to change.*

Figure 15.43 *Choose the desired alignment option and click Apply or OK.*

Figure 15.44 *The paragraph is aligned to the right.*

Figure 15.45 *On this page, the paragraph has been centered.*

Figure 15.46 *Select the paragraph(s) that you wish to convert to block quotes. (You don't have to select the entire paragraph.)*

Figure 15.47 *Choose any style you want in the Paragraph style pop-up menu. Then choose Block Quote in the Additional style pop-up menu.*

Figure 15.48 *The block quotes are indented on both sides.*

Creating a block quote

A block quote is a special device used on Web pages to call attention to a short paragraph. In Netscape, block quotes are formatted in the proportional font and are indented from both margins.

To create a block quote:

1. Click anywhere in the paragraph that you wish to make into a block quote **(Figure 15.46)**. It doesn't matter if the paragraph has any text in it yet.

2. Choose Text in the Properties menu. The Properties dialog box appears.

3. Click Paragraph to see the Paragraph Properties.

4. Choose the desired style in the Paragraph style pop-up menu.

5. Then choose Block Quote in the Additional style pop-up menu **(Figure 15.47)**.

6. If desired, choose an alignment option.

7. Click Apply to apply the changes without closing the dialog box. Change the options and click Apply again until you're satisfied.

8. Click OK (or Close if you've already applied the changes) to close the dialog box. The selected paragraph is changed to block quotes **(Fig. 15.48)**.

✔ Tips

■ You can combine block quotes with any other principal paragraph style.

■ In many browsers, block quotes are displayed in a fixed width font at a smaller size.

Creating a block quote

Applying many paragraph features at once

Although it's a bit easier to select the desired paragraph styles from the toolbar or the menu, the Paragraph Properties dialog box lets you apply several paragraph characteristics at once.

To apply several paragraph features at a time:

1. Place the cursor in the paragraph that you wish to modify. You don't need to select anything.

2. Choose Text in the Properties menu **(Figure 15.49)** to view the Properties dialog box.

3. Click the Paragraph tab to see the Paragraph Properties.

4. Choose the desired paragraph style, additional style, list styles, as well as an alignment **(Figure 15.50)**.

5. Click Apply to apply the changes without closing the dialog box. Make changes in the selections and click Apply again until you are satisfied.

6. Click OK (or Close if you've already applied the changes) to close the dialog box. The styles are applied.

✔ Tips

■ You can also make the Paragraph Properties appear by right clicking a paragraph and choosing Paragraph/ List properties in the submenu that appears **(Figure 15.51)**.

■ How do you eliminate styles? Since all paragraphs must have some style, simply apply a different one.

Figure 15.49 *Choose Text in the Properties menu.*

Figure 15.50 *Select the desired styles and click Apply or OK.*

Figure 15.51 *Right click anywhere in a paragraph to make the pop-up menu appear. Then choose Paragraph properties.*

Adding Images to a Page

Perhaps the greatest appeal of the World Wide Web and of HTML documents in particular is that they can contain colorful images. You can insert a photo of your cat on your personal home page, or a representation of your company's logo on your business page. And you can add images to link definitions, making buttons that take your reader to their next destination.

Image formats

Because the Web is accessed by all different kinds of computers, the graphics you use in your Web page must be in a format that each of these operating systems can recognize. The two most widely used formats are JPEG and GIF.

GIF, or Graphics Interchange Format, was developed by CompuServe. LZW, the compression it uses, reduces the size of images with large blocks of the same color—common in computer generated art. In addition, LZW is *lossless* compression. You can compress, uncompress, and recompress the image without any loss in quality.

The JPEG compression scheme is ideal for photographs and other "natural" color images. JPEG compressed images may have millions of colors, and their file size is determined primarily by their image size, not their number of colors.

However, JPEG is *lossy* compression— deciding that the eye cannot distinguish as many colors as are in your original image, it may eliminate them permanently to save space. Uncompressing the image will not restore the lost data.

Image formats

Inserting an image

Images add interest to your pages. They also make it slower to view. If you add too many images, readers will get frustrated with the download time. If you add too few, they may be bored. Balance is key.

To insert an image:

1. Click in the Editor window where you wish to insert the image **(Fig. 16.1)**.

2. Choose Image in the Insert menu **(Figure 16.2)**. The Image Properties dialog box appears.

3. Next to Image file name, click Browse **(Figure 16.3)**.

4. Locate the image that you wish to insert. Click Open. The image's file name appears in the Image Properties dialog box **(Figure 16.4)**.

5. Netscape will copy the image to the same directory that contains the page you are working on. If you don't want Netscape to do that, deselect the Copy image to the document's location checkbox at the bottom left corner of the dialog box.

6. Click OK. The image appears in the Editor window **(Figure 16.5)**.

✔ Tips

■ You can also click the Insert image button on the Character Properties toolbar to make the Image Properties dialog box appear.

■ You can quickly open an image in your preferred image editing software by clicking Edit image in the Image Properties dialog box. To choose the program, see page 254.

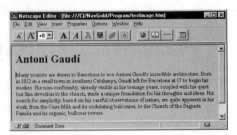

Figure 16.1 *Click in the Editor window where you wish the image to appear.*

Figure 16.2 *Choose Image in the Insert menu.*

Figure 16.3 *Click Browse next to the Image file name text box. (Or enter the file name manually.)*

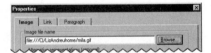

Figure 16.4 *The file name appears in the Image Properties dialog box. Click Close to exit.*

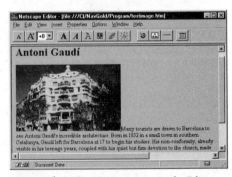

Figure 16.5 *The image appears in the Editor window at the insertion point, displacing text as necessary.*

Figure 16.6 *Select the image and then choose Image in the Properties menu.*

Figure 16.7 *Type the alternative text in the Text box under Alternative representations.*

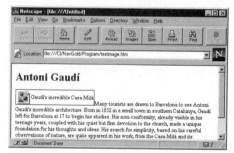

Figure 16.8 *Netscape users who have deactivated the Auto Load Images option and users of non-graphical browsers won't see the images, but will see the alternative text instead.*

Using alternative text

It's important to remember that not everyone who browses the World Wide Web uses Netscape to do it. Unix users, for example, typically use a program called Lynx, that does not show images at all. Users with a slow modem or computer may disable image viewing to speed up their browsing *(see page 33)*. In order to communicate what the images contain to those users who can't see them on the page, you can use alternative text which appears when the images don't.

To use alternative text:

1. If you are inserting a new image, follow steps 1–4 on page 190. For an existing image, select the image and choose Image in the Properties menu **(Figure 16.6)**. The Image Properties dialog box appears.

2. In the Image Properties dialog box, under Alternate representations, type the alternative text in the Text box **(Figure 16.7)**.

3. Click OK to close the Image Properties dialog box. The effect is not readily seen in Netscape's browser until you deselect the Auto Load Images option **(Figure 16.8)**.

✔ Tips

■ Users who disable automatic image loading to save time can sometimes be enticed into loading your images if you use *descriptive* alternative text.

■ If you use images as navigational buttons, it is essential to use alternative text. Otherwise, the user who doesn't view images will be unable to navigate on your page.

Using low resolution images to speed viewing

Low resolution images load faster than high resolution images. You can specify a low resolution version of your image to load immediately while the high resolution is coming in slowly. This way, your reader gets instant feedback.

To use a low resolution image:

1. If you are inserting a new image, follow steps 1–4 on page 190. For an existing image, select the image and choose Image in the Properties menu. The Image Properties dialog box appears.

2. In the Image text box under Alternative representations, type the path and file name of the low resolution version of the image, or click Browse to locate it on your hard disk **(Figure 16.9)**.

3. Click OK to close the Image Properties dialog box.

Figure 16.9 *In the Image text box under Alternative representations, type the file name and path of the low resolution version of your image. Or click Browse to locate the file on your hard disk.*

Image size

If you've wandered a bit around the Internet, you are sure to have experienced The Page From Hell. The designer was so anxious to show you every image he's every created, that he placed them all on the same page. And no small images either—these are 24 bit color images. You're still on a 14.4 modem, but that's no excuse to make you wait this long to see the page. After a minute or two staring at the progress indicator at the bottom of the browser, you bag, and surf to a friendlier page.

When you construct *your* page, make sure you keep your entire page to under 30K—including images. It will take your users with 14.4 modems, not to mention those who are still on 9600s, about a second to load each K of data, for a total of 30 seconds. That's about how long you can expect anyone to wait.

If you want to include larger images, you have several options. First, you can use a miniature version, or icon, of the image on your page that links the user—if they so choose—to the full image. Next, you can create a low resolution version of the image that loads almost immediately and allows the user to browse the text areas of your page while the high resolution image is loading *(see page 192)*. Finally, you can interlace the image which also lets the user browse almost immediately as the image gradually comes into focus. If your pages are still very slow, try dividing your images among several pages.

Why the resolution is not so important

Since most monitors display everything at 72 or 96 dpi, there is no reason to save your images with a higher resolution, unless you want your users to be able to download and print your images at the other end. Generally, that's not necessary, and the higher resolution only guarantees longer download times.

Why the number of colors *is* so important

Although many Macintoshes and some higher-end monitors for PCs can show thousands or even millions of colors on the screen at once, the vast majority of users are limited to 256 colors. This means that if you create several images and each uses its own set of 256 colors, the images will not appear correctly. Therefore, if you plan to include several images on a single page, you need to be careful to either limit each image to 50 or so colors, or to use the same set of colors for all the images.

In addition, the fewer the colors in your image, the smaller the file size, and thus the faster the download time. To create a fast, friendly Web page, keep your color count down to a minimum.

Image size, resolution, and colors

Wrapping text around images

Thanks to Netscape and its extensions, you can wrap text around images, making for a more visually interesting page. Beware, many other browsers do not support text wrap.

To wrap text around images:

1. If you are inserting a new image, follow steps 1–4 on page 190. For an existing image, select the image and choose Image in the Properties menu. The Image Properties dialog box appears.

2. Netscape considers text wrap a kind of alignment. Click the desired text wrap option (either to the right of the image or to the left of the image) in the Alignment section of the Image Properties dialog box **(Figure 16.10)**.

3. Click OK to close the dialog box. Text wrap is not shown in the Editor window **(Figure 16.11)**.

4. To view the results, choose Browse window in the File menu or click the View in Browser button 🖼. In the browser, the text is shown wrapped around the image **(Figure 16.12)**.

✔ Tips

■ Insert an image *before* (that is, above or to the left of) the text you want to wrap around it.

■ You can also regulate the amount of space between the image and the text. For more information, consult *Adding space around an image* on page 196.

Figure 16.10 *Choose one of the two text wrap options in the Alignment area of the Image Properties dialog box.*

Figure 16.11 *Text wrap is not shown in the Editor window.*

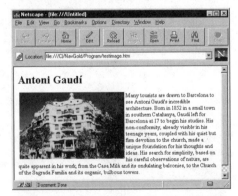

Figure 16.12 *Choose Browse Document in the File menu to view the page in the browser where the text wrap is visible.*

Figure 16.13 *Place the insertion point where you want to stop the text from wrapping. Here, the cursor is in front of "His nonconformity..." in the third line.*

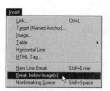

Figure 16.14 *Choose Break below Image(s) in the Insert menu.*

Figure 16.15 *Since text wrap is not visible in the Editor window, it's hard to see how the break affects the final look of the page.*

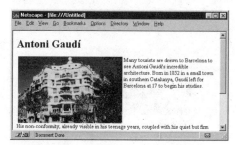

Figure 16.16 *In the browser, the break makes the text stop flowing until it reaches the end of the image.*

Stopping text wrap

Once you tell Netscape to wrap text around an image, it does so until it runs out of text—or encounters a break. You can insert a manual break, as needed.

To stop text wrap:

1. Place the insertion point where you want the text to stop wrapping **(Figure 16.13)**.

2. Choose Break below Image(s) in the Insert menu **(Figure 16.14)**. In the Editor window, you will see a line break **(Figure 16.15)**. In the browser, the text will stop flowing and won't begin again until below the image **(Figure 16.16)**.

Adding space around an image

When you wrap text around images, the image is sometimes squashed or crowded by the text. You can remedy this effect by adding extra space around the image.

To add space around an image:

1. If you are inserting a new image, follow steps 1–4 on page 190. For an existing image, select the image and choose Image in the Properties menu. The Image Properties dialog box appears.

2. Enter the amount of space, in pixels, that you wish to leave around the image in the Left and right and Top and bottom text boxes in the Space around image section **(Figure 16.18)**.

3. Click OK to close the Image Properties dialog box. Although the added space is theoretically visible in the Editor window, you can get a better picture in the browser where the text is wrapped as well.

4. Choose Browse Document in the File window or click the View in Browser button on the File/Edit Tools toolbar. You may be asked to save the page. Click OK to do so. The page is shown as it will appear on the Web **(Figure 16.19)**.

✔ Tip

■ Unfortunately, in Netscape Gold (or indeed in HTML), there's no way to add space on just one side of an image (e.g., the text side). One solution is to add the space in Photoshop, and then make it transparent.

Figure 16.17 *Another way to make the Image Properties dialog box is appear is to right click an image and choose Image Properties in the menu.*

Figure 16.18 *Enter the amount of space—in pixels—that you want to create around the image.*

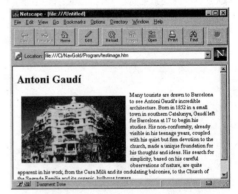

Figure 16.19 *Now the image is not jammed up next to the text. Notice also how space has been added to all sides of the image. Compare this illustration with Figure 16.12 on page 194.*

Figure 16.20 *Right click an image and choose Image Properties in the pop-up menu.*

Figure 16.21 *Enter the desired size, in pixels, for the image in the Dimensions area.*

Figure 16.22 *In this example, the image has been reduced to half its size.*

Figure 16.23 *You can distort an image by entering non-proportional dimensions.*

Changing the display size of an image

One of Netscape Gold's advantages is that it automatically includes the size of the image in your Web page, according to the image's real dimensions. This allows the browser to allocate the necessary space for the image as it is downloaded and to display the surrounding text immediately. You can also use the size coordinates to change the display of the image on the page.

To change the display size of an image:

1. If you are inserting a new image, follow steps 1–4 on page 190. For an existing image, select the image and choose Image in the Properties menu. The Image Properties dialog box appears.

2. Enter the desired size for the image in the Dimensions area **(Figure 16.21)**.

3. If desired, click Apply to apply the changes without closing the dialog box. Adjust the dimensions and click Apply again until you are satisfied.

4. Click OK (or close if you've already applied the changes) to close the Image Properties dialog box. The changes are shown immediately in the Editor window **(Figure 16.22)**.

✔ Tips

■ To return an image to its original size, click Original Size in the Dimensions area of the Image Properties box.

■ You can distort an image by entering non-proportional dimensions **(Figure 16.23)**.

Creating a border around an image

To set off an image from the surrounding elements on the page, you can create a border around it.

To create a border around an image:

1. If you are inserting a new image, follow steps 1–4 on page 190. For an existing image, select the image and choose Image in the Properties menu. The Image Properties dialog box appears.

2. Enter the width of the border, in pixels, in the Solid border text box in the Space around image area **(Figure 16.24)**.

3. If desired, click Apply to apply the changes without closing the dialog box. Adjust the width and click Apply again until you are satisfied with the results.

4. Click OK (or close if you've already applied the changes) to close the Image Properties dialog box. The border is shown immediately in the Editor window **(Figure 16.25)**.

Figure 16.24 *Enter the border thickness in pixels.*

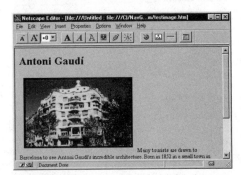

Figure 16.25 *The image appears with a 5-pixel wide border.*

Figure 16.26 *This is a 10-pixel wide border.*

Figure 16.27 *Select an alignment option (one of the first five icons in the Alignment section) in the Image Properties dialog box.*

Figure 16.28 *This image is aligned with the top line of text (the first Alignment option, as shown in Figure 16.27). Notice that only the first line of text is affected.*

Figure 16.29 *The middle of this image is aligned with the middle of the first line of text (which is the second Alignment option).*

Aligning images

Images can be aligned in several different ways, depending on what effect you're trying to create. The only thing you can't do is align an image and wrap text around it at the same time.

To align an image:

1. If you are inserting a new image, follow steps 1–4 on page 190. For an existing image, select the image and choose Image in the Properties menu. The Image Properties dialog box appears.

2. Choose one of the first five options in the Alignment area **(Figure 16.27)**. (The last two are for text wrap; see page 194.)

3. If desired, click Apply to apply the changes without closing the dialog box. Choose a different alignment option and click Apply again until you are satisfied with the results.

4. Click OK (or Close if you've already applied the changes) to close the Image Properties dialog box. The image is immediately aligned in the Editor window **(Figure 16.28)**.

✔ Tips

■ The alignment option you choose only affects the first line of text.

■ If you have several images on the same line, you can align them in different ways.

■ For more information about wrapping text around images (using the last two icons in the Alignment section), consult *Wrapping text around images* on page 194.

Adding a horizontal line

Horizontal lines are amazingly useful for dividing Web pages into intelligible chunks of information. Netscape lets you control the size, width, and shading of horizontal lines, but most other browsers don't recognize these fancy additions.

To add a horizontal line:

1. Click in the Editor window where you wish to insert the horizontal line **(Figure 16.30)**.

2. Choose Horizontal Line in the Insert menu **(Figure 16.31)**. The default style line is inserted **(Figure 16.32)**.

3. If desired, change the line as described on page 201.

✔ Tips

■ You can also insert a new horizontal line by clicking the Insert Horizontal Line button on the Character Properties toolbar.

■ Eliminate a horizontal line by selecting it and pressing Backspace.

Figure 16.30 *Click in the Editor window where you wish the line to appear.*

Figure 16.31 *Choose Horizontal line in the Insert menu.*

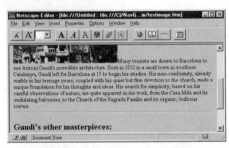

Figure 16.32 *The default horizontal line is 2 pixels high, as wide as the window, and uses 3-D shading (at least in Netscape's browser).*

Figure 16.33 *Choose Horizontal Line in the Properties menu.*

Figure 16.34 *Choose the desired options for the horizontal line and click OK.*

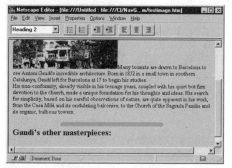

Figure 16.35 *This line is 10 pixels high, 50% of the width of the window, and centered. It does not use 3-D shading.*

Changing a horizontal line

Netscape has added several options to its horizontal lines. You can adjust a line's thickness (height), width—both as a percentage of the window width and in absolute pixels—alignment, and shading.

To change a horizontal line:

1. Select the line and choose Horizontal Line in the Properties menu (**Figure 16.33**). The Horizontal Line Properties dialog box appears.

2. Choose a height (thickness) in pixels, for the line (**Figure 16.34**).

3. Enter a number for the width of the line, either as a percentage of the total window size, or in absolute terms, in pixels.

4. If you've chosen a line width that is narrower than the window width, choose an alignment.

5. Finally, you can choose to add 3-D shading for the line or to leave it in black and white.

6. Click OK to save the changes. The results are shown in the Editor window (**Figure 16.35**).

✔ Tips

■ Right click a line and choose Horizontal Line Properties in the pop-up menu to access the Horizontal Line Properties dialog box.

■ Selecting a line and clicking the Horizontal Line button ▬ on the toolbar *should* make the Horizontal Line Properties dialog box appear. It doesn't; it simply inserts a new line.

Changing a horizontal line

Choosing colors and/or a background image

You can set your own default colors for text, new links, active links, and visited links. You can also choose a color or an image for the background. Although it's rather in vogue to use garish colors on the Web, it also makes the page hard to read.

To choose a page's colors and/or background image:

1. Choose Document in the Properties menu **(Figure 16.36)**. The Document Properties dialog box appears.

2. In the Custom Colors section, click the element whose color you wish to change. The Color dialog box appears. Choose a color and click OK.

3. In the Background image section, check Use Image and then click Browse for File to choose a background image **(Figure 16.37)**.

4. Click OK to close the Document Properties dialog box.

✔ Tips

■ Netscape includes a series of "color schemes" in the Color Schemes pop-up menu. You can choose one of these color schemes and then modify it as desired.

■ A preview of your choices is always shown at the right of the Custom Colors section in the dialog box.

■ If the image is smaller than the page, it will be tiled to fill the background.

■ If you choose a background color before choosing a background image, both will be used.

Figure 16.36 *Choose Document in the Properties menu.*

Figure 16.37 *Choose colors for the different elements. Choose between a color and an image for the background. Then click OK to save the changes.*

Figure 16.38 *If the image is smaller than the page, it will be tiled to cover the background.*

Choosing colors and/or a background

Creating Links in a Page

17

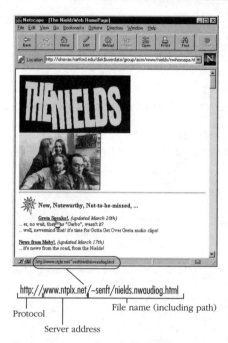

http://www.ntplx.net/~senft/nields.nwaudiog.html

Protocol

Server address

File name (including path)

Figure 17.1 *Place the pointer over a link and its URL becomes visible in the status bar at the bottom of the window. If the Location bar is visible, it will display the URL of the page you're currently viewing.*

As discussed in Chapter 2, *Surfing the Web*, a Web page can contain dynamic connections with other Web pages, enabling users to jump from one page to another in search of information. These connections are called *links*.

A link can bring the user to the top of a Web page or to a specific section of that page, to an FTP or Gopher site, to a newsgroup, or even to an e-mail address. The Web page designer decides where the link will go.

Links and URLs

Links are made out of URLs, or *Uniform Resource Locators*. The URL is an address that gives the exact location on the Internet of a link's destination. A URL is comprised of a protocol, a server name and a file name, including the path **(Fig. 17.1)**. The protocol defines what kind of connection will be made (Web, FTP, Gopher, Mail, etc.). The server name is the official name, or IP address, of the server that contains the desired file. The file name is the exact name, including the path indicating its location on the server, of the desired file.

Every single piece of information on the Internet—every page, every image, every file—has a unique URL. Thus, when a user clicks a link, Netscape knows exactly where to go to find the information and display it.

In addition to the URL, a link has *display text*, that is, the text that will be underlined and in blue (in most cases) and that indicates the content of the link to the user.

Links and URLs

Copying a link from another source

The pages you find on the Web already contain many interesting links, to other pages, FTP and Gopher sites, e-mail addresses and newsgroups. You may also find good links in e-mail you receive or in news postings. Or you may wish to include links from your Bookmarks collection. You can copy any link you find and insert it on your own page.

To copy a link from another source:

1. Open the page you are designing in the Editor window and place the cursor where you want the link to appear **(Figure 17.2)**.

2. Open the browser, Mail, News or Bookmark window and the document that contains the link you wish to copy **(Figure 17.3)**.

3. Organize the two windows on your screen so that the link is visible on the browser window and a piece of the Editor window is also visible.

4. Click the link and drag it to the Editor window. The browser window becomes active. When the icon is over the Editor window and gains a plus sign, let go **(Figure 17.4)**.

5. Click the Editor window to make it active. The link is added at the insertion point. The display text is the same as it was on the original page **(Figure 17.5)**.

6. If desired, select the display text and change it to something more descriptive or specific **(Figure 17.6)**.

Figure 17.2 *Click in the Editor window where you wish the link to appear.*

Figure 17.3 *In the browser, navigate to the page that has the link you want to copy.*

Figure 17.4 *Drag the link from the browser to the Editor window. When the cursor shows the link icon and a plus sign, let go of the mouse button.*

Figure 17.5 *The link is added to the page in the Editor window, with the same display text it had on the original page.*

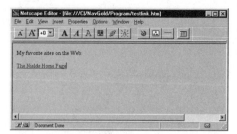

Figure 17.6 *Select the link and type over it to change the display text to something slightly more intelligible, if necessary.*

Figure 17.7 *To copy a link of the page you're currently browsing and not a link it contains, drag the Link icon (at the left of the Location text box) to the Editor window.*

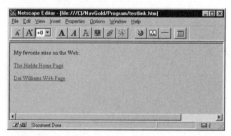

Figure 17.8 *When you use the Link icon, the title of the page you're browsing is used as display text for the link.*

✔ **Tips**

- To insert a link to the *current* page showing in the browser, whether it be a remote page on another server or a local file on your hard disk, drag the Current Page Link button 🖉 at the left of the Location text box to the desired spot in the Editor window **(Figure 17.7 and Figure 17.8)**.

- If you prefer, double click the Current Page Link icon 🖉 to copy the page's URL to the clipboard and then paste it in the Link Properties dialog box manually *(see page 206)*. If you don't see the Current Page Link icon or the Location text box, you'll have to make them visible *(see page 19)*.

- If the Editor window isn't hidden by the document that contains the link, you'll be able to see the insertion point and choose where you want to "drop" the copied link.

- If you try to drag a *folder* from the Bookmarks window, the URL of the first item is copied to the Editor window in text form instead of as a link.

- You can't drag an address from the Address Book to create an e-mail link. Instead, either open the Address Book as a Web page *(see page 140)* and drag links from there or enter the address manually *(see page 206)*.

- Once you create a link on a page, you can test it by right clicking the link and choosing Browse to [link address] in the pop-up menu that appears. You can edit the linked page by right clicking the link and choosing Open Link in Editor in the pop-up menu.

Copying a link from another source

Creating a link manually

If the link doesn't already exist on another page or if you want to create a link without browsing the page (perhaps you don't want to open your Internet connection), you can type the link's URL manually.

To create a link manually:

1. Click in the Editor window where you want the link to appear.

2. Choose Link in the Insert menu **(Figure 17.9)**. The Insert Link dialog box appears.

3. Type the display text in the Link source text box **(Figure 17.10)**.

4. Type or copy the URL for the link in the Link to box. If the link will be to a local page on your hard disk, click Browse File and find the desired page.

5. Click OK. The link appears in the Editor window **(Figure 17.11)**.

✔ Tip

■ If you don't type any display text in the Link source text box, Netscape uses the URL address as display text.

Figure 17.9 *Click in the Editor window where you want the link to appear and then choose Link in the Insert menu.*

Figure 17.10 *Type the display text in the Link source text box and the URL for the link in the Link to text box. Then click OK.*

Figure 17.11 *The link appears in the Editor window as defined.*

Figure 17.12 *Select the desired text.*

Figure 17.13 *The selected text is automatically entered as display text.*

Figure 17.14 *Enter the URL for the link.*

Figure 17.15 *The text is converted into a link.*

If the display text already exists and you simply want to add a link to it, there is an easier way.

To create a link manually from existing text:

1. Select the text that you want to make a link out of **(Figure 17.12)**.

2. Choose Link in the Insert menu. The Link Properties dialog box appears with the display text automatically inserted **(Figure 17.13)**.

3. Type the URL for the link or click Browse if the link is to a local file on your hard disk **(Figure 17.14)**.

4. Click OK. The selected text is now a link **(Figure 17.15)**.

✔ Tips

■ You can insert any kind of URL in the Link to a page location text box, including URLs for Web pages, FTP or Gopher sites, e-mail addresses and newsgroups or newsgroup postings. Links to Web sites should be in the form: **http://www.site.com/path/page.html**. Links to FTP sites should resemble **ftp://ftp.site.com/path/**. Links to Gopher sites should look like **gopher://gophersite.edu/path/**. The format for links to e-mail addresses is **mailto:name@site.com**. The format for links to newsgroups is **news:newsgroup.name**.

■ You can also right click a selection (or insertion point) in the Editor window and then choose Create Link using selected (or Insert new Link if you had nothing selected). The Link Properties dialog box appears and you continue as described above.

Creating a target

The simplest kind of link brings the user to the *top* of a Web page. If you want a link to bring the user to a *specific part* of the page, you have to create a target and then point the link at that target.

To create a target:

1. Select the text in the Editor window that you want to appear at the top of the browser window when the user clicks the link **(Figure 17.16)**. This is the target.

2. Choose Target (Named Anchor) in the Insert menu **(Figure 17.17)**. The Target Properties dialog box appears.

3. The text box automatically contains the text you selected in step 1. Either accept that word or type another that identifies this section of the Web page you are designing and click OK **(Figure 17.18)**.

4. A small target icon appears next to the selected text **(Figure 17.19)**. You can now create a link that connects to this target.

✔ Tips

■ To create a link that points to the target, consult *Linking to a target on the same page* on page 209 or *Linking to a target on a different page* on page 210.

■ The target icon is not visible when the page is viewed in a browser.

■ You can also insert a target by clicking the Insert Target (Named Anchor) button on the File/Edit Tools toolbar.

Figure 17.16 *Click in the area that should appear at the top of the page when the user clicks the targeted link.*

Figure 17.17 *Choose Target (Named Anchor) in the Insert menu.*

Figure 17.18 *Type a name for the target. Any text selected at the beginning is automatically entered here.*

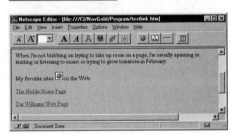

Figure 17.19 *A target icon is inserted next to the selected text.*

Figure 17.20 *Select the text that you want to convert into a link (or click where you wish to insert a link).*

Figure 17.21 *In the Link Properties dialog box, click Current Document and then select the desired target for the link in the list.*

Figure 17.22 *The link is created.*

Figure 17.23 *When the user clicks the targeted link, the corresponding section of the page is displayed at the top of the browser.*

Linking to a target on the same page

If you have a particularly long Web page, you can create a kind of table of contents at the top of the page. Then set up each entry as a link to the section farther down on the page with targets.

To create a link to a target on the same page:

1. Click in the Editor window where you want to create the link. If desired, select the text you want to convert into display text for the link **(Fig. 17.20)**.

2. Choose Link in the Insert menu. The Link Properties dialog box appears.

3. If necessary, type the display text at the top of the dialog box.

4. Choose the desired target in the scroll list in the Link to area. The target name appears, preceded by a pound sign (#), in the Link to text box **(Figure 17.21)**.

5. Click OK. The link appears in the Editor window **(Figure 17.22)**.

✔ Tips

■ You can also access the Link Properties dialog box by right clicking with the mouse and then choosing Insert new Link in the submenu. Or, click the Make Link button 🖉 on the Character Properties toolbar.

■ If you select text before choosing the Link command, the selected text is automatically entered as display text.

Linking to a target on a different page

Once you've created a target in one of your Web pages, you can create a link to it. The link can be on the same page (as in a table of contents) or from another page. Since you can't create targets in e-mail addresses, FTP or Gopher sites, or newsgroups or postings, a link to a target must be to a Web page.

Figure 17.24 *Right click the link and select Link Properties in the pop-up menu.*

To create a link to a target on a different page:

1. Create a link to the remote page *(see pages 204 and 206)*.

2. Right click the link and select Link Properties in the pop-up menu or click the Make Link button ![button] on the toolbar **(Figure 17.24)**. The Link Properties box appears with the display text and URL already entered.

3. Under Show targets in, choose Selected File **(Figure 17.25)**.

4. Choose the desired target in the list. It is automatically appended to the URL, separated by a number symbol (#) **(Figure 17.26)**.

5. Click OK to save the changes.

✔ Tip

■ You can create the link at the same time you select the target, by entering all the information manually, but it's not as easy.

Figure 17.25 *When you open the Link Properties dialog box, the URL appears in the Link to text box while a list of possible targets appears.*

Figure 17.26 *When you choose a target, its name is appended to the URL, separated by a # sign.*

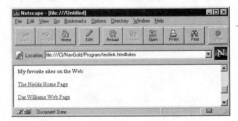

Figure 17.27 *When the user clicks the targeted link, the corresponding section of the page is displayed.*

Figure 17.28 *Add the image to the page and select it.*

Figure 17.29 *Choose Link in the Insert menu.*

Figure 17.30 *Type or copy the URL in the Link to text area. Choose a target if desired.*

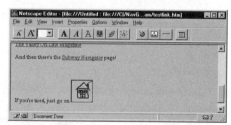

Figure 17.31 *The linked image is shown with a blue frame.*

Creating a link to an image

To add navigational buttons to your page, you have to first insert an image and then make it into a link.

To create a link to an image:

1. Add the image to the page in the Editor window *(see page 190)* and select it **(Figure 17.28)**.

2. Choose Link in the Insert menu **(Figure 17.29)**. The Link Properties dialog box appears with the image's file name in the Link source area.

3. Type the URL for the link in the Link to text box, or click Browse if the link is to a local file on your hard disk **(Figure 17.30)**.

4. Select a target for the link, if desired *(see page 209)*.

5. Click OK to close the Link Properties dialog box. The image now appears with a blue border to show that it is a link **(Figure 17.31)**.

✔ Tips

■ You can also right click the image and then choose Create Link using selected in the pop-up menu to make the Link Properties dialog box appear for the image.

■ Or, you can select the image and then click the Make Link button on the Character Properties toolbar to open the Link Properties dialog box for the image.

Creating a link to an image

Changing or removing a link

As you design a Web page, you will find that every so often you need to update a link or add a target to it—or get rid of it.

To change or delete a link:

1. Select the link you want to change **(Figure 17.32)**.

2. Choose Link in the Properties menu **(Figure 17.33)**. The Link Properties dialog box appears **(Figure 17.34)**.

3. Change the URL or target *(see pages 206 and 208)* or click Remove Link to make the link into regular text.

4. Click OK to save the changes.

✔ Tips

■ To change a link's display text, simply select the text and type something else.

■ Another way to eliminate the link properties from text is by selecting the link and choosing Remove Links in the Properties menu. Or right click a link and choose Remove Link in the pop-up menu. The display text remains.

■ To eliminate a link *and* its display text, select it and press Backspace.

■ You can also make the Link Properties dialog box appear by right clicking the link and choosing Link properties in the pop-up menu **(Figure 17.35)** or by selecting the link and clicking the Make Link button .

Figure 17.32 *Select the link you want to change.*

Figure 17.33 *Choose Link in the Properties menu.*

Figure 17.34 *Make any necessary changes to the URL or to the target. Or click Remove Link to remove the link information from the text. Click OK to save the changes.*

Figure 17.35 *Right click the link and choose Link properties in the pop-up menu to make the Link Properties dialog box (Figure 17.34) appear.*

Figure 18.1 *Detailed lists are often best displayed in a table.*

Figure 18.2 *Tables often look slightly more compact when viewed with Netscape's browser.*

Detailed lists with categorized information are infinitely easier to understand in table format. With Netscape Gold's new tables feature, they're *almost* simple to create—certainly much easier than constructing them by hand.

If you are worried about users who use a browser that doesn't understand tables, you might consider creating hand spaced tables with preformatted text *(see page 181)*. Tables made with preformatted text can be read by *any* browser.

✔ Note

■ Throughout this chapter, you'll learn all the techniques for editing tables. In each technique you have two choices. Either select the part of the table you wish to edit, choose Table in the Properties menu, and then click the appropriate tab for the item that you wish to modify. Or right click the element that you wish to change and choose Table properties in the pop-up menu. The appropriate tab will appear automatically in the Table Properties dialog box. To save space, only one method is discussed in each technique, but they can be used interchangeably.

Creating tables

Creating a new table

You can create a new table in any part of your Web page. The table will appear at the insertion point.

To create a new table:

1. Click on the page where you wish to insert the table **(Figure 18.3)**.

2. Choose Table in the Table submenu under the Insert menu **(Figure 18.4)**. The New Table Properties dialog box appears **(Figure 18.5)**.

3. Define how many rows and columns the table should have by entering numbers in the Number of rows and Number of columns boxes.

4. If desired, check the Table width box and leave the percentage at 100%. This makes setting up the table a lot easier.

5. If desired, further define the appearance of the table as described in the rest of this chapter.

6. Click OK. The empty table is added to your page **(Figure 18.6)**.

✔ Tips

■ For information on filling your table, consult *Entering text in a table* on page 217.

■ You can also insert a table by clicking the Insert Table icon on the Character Format toolbar.

Figure 18.3 *Click in the part of your page where you wish to insert the table and then click the Insert table button on the Character Properties toolbar.*

Figure 18.4 *Or choose Table in the Table submenu under Insert.*

Figure 18.5 *Enter the desired values in the New Table Properties dialog box and then click OK to insert the table in your page.*

Figure 18.6 *The empty table appears on your page. Note that the right column is stretched to fit the window. It will be adjusted automatically as you fill the table with text.*

Figure 18.7 *Click in the cell that you wish to span more than one column (or row).*

Figure 18.8 *Choose Table in the Properties menu.*

Figure 18.9 *Enter the number of rows or columns the cell should span at the top of the Cell tab.*

Figure 18.10 *The selected cell now spans two columns. Meanwhile, an extra cell is pushed out to the right and will have to be deleted.*

Spanning a cell over columns or rows

If you have a lot of information that you wish to convey with a table, you can divide a table header into several categories by having it span several columns (or rows), and adding more specific headers in the row below (or column to the right).

To span a cell over several rows and/or columns:

1. Click in the desired cell **(Figure 18.7)**.

2. Select Table in the Properties menu **(Figure 18.8)** and click Cell in the Table Properties dialog box that appears.

3. Enter the number of rows and columns that the cell should span next to Cell spans at the top of the dialog box **(Figure 18.9)**.

4. If desired, click the Apply button to see how the changes affect the table. Repeat step 3 and click Apply until you are satisfied with the results.

5. Click OK to close the dialog box. The cell spans the appropriate number of columns **(Figure 18.10)**.

✔ Tip

■ When you make a cell span more than one row or column, you may find there are extra cells that need to be deleted. Simply right click them and choose Cell under Delete in the pop-up menu that appears or consult *Adding or deleting cells, rows, or columns* on page 216 for more details.

Spanning a cell over columns or rows

215

Adding or deleting cells, rows, or columns

Unless you completely design the table on paper before opening Netscape's Editor window, it's almost impossible to know exactly how many cells, rows, or columns you'll need. Luckily, you can add and delete them as you go along.

To add parts of a table:

1. Click in the table where the new cell, row or column should be inserted.

2. Choose Row, Column, or Cell in the Table submenu of the Insert menu. The desired element is inserted.

To delete parts of a table:

1. Click in the undesired element **(Figure 18.11)**.

2. Choose Table, Row, Column, or Cell in the Delete Table submenu in the Edit menu. The selected part disappears **(Figure 18.12)**.

✔ Tips

■ As shown in the illustration, you can also right click an element and then choose Table, Row, Column, or Cell in the Insert or Delete submenus of the pop-up menu that appears.

■ There is no warning when you delete part of a table. Choose Undo in the Edit menu (Ctrl+Z) to get it back.

■ Elements are added to the right or below the current item. Thus, the only way to add a cell *before another* is to create a new cell below or after it and then copy and paste the contents into the new location.

Figure 18.11 *Right click the cell, row or column that you wish to eliminate and then choose Delete in the pop-up menu and the type of element in the submenu. In this example, we eliminate the extra cell created when we spanned a cell over two columns on the previous page.*

Figure 18.12 *The extra cell disappears.*

Adding or deleting cells, rows, or columns

Figure 18.13 *Once you've adjusted the cells so that they span the desired number of rows or columns, you're ready to enter text in the table. Simply click in the desired cell and type. Use the arrow keys to move from cell to cell—not Tab.*

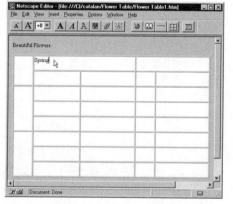

Figure 18.14 *By default, the text will appear aligned to the left and at the same size and style as regular body text.*

Entering text in a table

Since you can't create a table out of existing text, you'll have to enter text in the table after creating it.

To enter text in a table:

1. Click in the cell in which you wish to enter information **(Figure 18.13)**.

2. Type the desired contents. The cell automatically expands to fit the text **(Figure 18.14)**.

3. Use the mouse or the left and right arrow keys to move to the next cell.

4. Repeat steps 2 and 3 until the table is complete.

✔ Tips

■ You may add new cells, rows or columns at any time. For more information, consult *Adding or deleting cells, rows, or columns* on page 216.

■ The most natural thing is to want to use the Tab key to move from cell to cell. It doesn't work. Worse yet, it adds big indents to the contents of your cell and you can't get rid of them by backspacing. Instead, to eliminate the indents, click the Decrease Indent icon on the Paragraph Format toolbar.

■ As you enter information into the table, the cells may widen or narrow to fit the contents. This is normal.

Entering text in a table

Formatting a table's headers

Although you can manually add physical formatting like bold and italics to distinguish a table's headers from its contents, you're better off formatting them as headers. This way, any browser that understands tables will be able to interpret and distinguish the headers correctly.

To format a table's headers:

1. Click in the cell that contains the header text **(Figure 18.15)**.

2. Choose Table in the Properties menu and then click the Row tab in the Table Properties dialog box that appears.

3. Click Header style in the Text section at the right of the dialog box **(Figure 18.16)**.

4. If desired, click the Apply button at the bottom of the dialog box to see the changes.

5. Click OK to close the dialog box and save the changes **(Figure 18.17)**.

✔ Tips

■ You can only format one cell at a time. If you select more than one, only the first cell is affected.

■ Right click a cell and choose Table properties in the pop-up menu to view the Table Properties dialog box.

■ Different browsers display headers in different ways. While Netscape shows headers in boldface and centered in the cell, Mosaic, to give one example, aligns header cells to the left, while also displaying them in boldface.

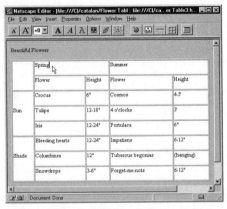

Figure 18.15 *Click in the cell that you wish to define as a table header.*

Figure 18.16 *In the Table Properties dialog box, check the Header style box in the Text section.*

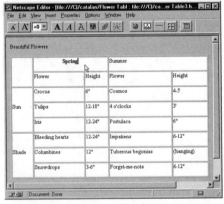

Figure 18.17 *Netscape displays header cells in boldface and centered. Other browsers may display them differently.*

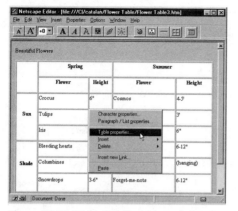

Figure 18.18 *Right click the table and choose Table properties in the pop-up menu.*

Figure 18.19 *Enter the desired width in pixels in the Border line width box in the Table Properties dialog box.*

Figure 18.20 *Netscape shades the border, according to the background color. Other browsers may display the border differently.*

Defining a table's border

Giving your table a border helps separate it from the rest of the text.

To define a border:

1. Click anywhere in the table to select it **(Figure 18.18)**.

2. Choose Table from the Properties menu and click the Table tab to see the Table Properties dialog box.

3. Enter the desired width for the border, in pixels, next to Border line width at the top of the dialog box **(Fig. 18.19)**.

4. If desired, click Apply to see the effect of the changes. Make further changes as desired until you're satisfied.

5. Click OK to save the changes and close the dialog box **(Figure 18.20)**.

✔ Tips

■ To eliminate the border, enter a value of 0 in the Border line width box.

■ You can define the width of the border when you initially create the table.

■ As shown in the illustration, right click a table and choose Table Properties in the pop-up menu to view the Table Properties dialog box.

■ It doesn't matter where you place the insertion point. Changing the border affects the entire table.

Defining a table's border

Adding a caption

A caption gives a short description of a table's contents. By adding this information in the form of a caption, it will always be related and connected to the table, regardless of the browser used to view it.

To add a caption:

1. Click anywhere in the table to select it **(Figure 18.21)**.

2. Choose Table in the Properties menu and then click the Table tab to see the Table attributes.

3. Check the Include caption option at the bottom of the dialog box **(Figure 18.22)**.

4. Check the above or below table options to determine the position of the caption.

5. Click Apply to see the effect of the changes. Change the options and click Apply again until you are satisfied.

6. Click OK to save the changes and close the dialog box. The cursor is automatically positioned in the caption area on your page.

7. Type the caption **(Figure 18.23)**.

✔ Tips

■ Different browsers display captions in different ways. While Netscape centers captions and divides the lines to fit the table's width, Mosaic displays captions in boldface and aligns them to the left.

■ If your table already contains a caption, you can use this technique to move the caption above (or below) the table.

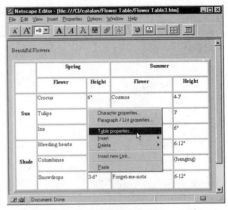

Figure 18.21 *Right click the table and choose Table properties in the pop-up menu.*

Figure 18.22 *Check the Include caption box and then mark either the above or the below table radio button to determine the caption's position.*

Figure 18.23 *Once you close the Table Properties dialog box, the insertion point will be automatically placed in the caption area. Type the caption.*

Figure 18.24 *Enter the desired values in the Cell spacing and Cell padding boxes to determine the amount of space that should be added between and inside the cells.*

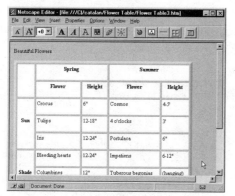

Figure 18.25 *Increasing cell spacing thickens the borders between cells; increasing cell padding adds invisible space between the contents of the cell and the cell's borders.*

Spacing and padding cells

Cell spacing is the amount of space between individual cells. You can sometimes make a table easier to read by adjusting the cell spacing.

To add cell spacing or padding:

1. Click anywhere in the table to select it.

2. Select Table in the Properties menu and then click the Table tab.

3. In the Cell spacing box, enter the amount of space, in pixels, that should appear between one cell and the next **(Figure 18.24)**.

4. In the Cell padding box, enter the amount of space, in pixels, that should appear between the cells contents and the border of the cell.

5. Click the Apply button to see the changes. Make additional changes and click Apply until you're satisfied with the results.

6. Click OK to close the dialog box and save the changes to the table **(Figure 18.25)**.

✔ Tips

■ The alignment options consider the cell padding as the actual cell limits, and thus may give unexpected results.

■ The default value for cell spacing is 2 pixels. The default value for cell padding is 1 pixel.

Spacing and padding cells

Changing the table's width and height

Every person who jumps to your page on the Web may see your table at a different size, depending on the size of the window he or she is using. You can set a minimum height and width for the table, if desired.

To change the width and height of a table:

1. Select the table and choose Table in the Properties menu or right click the table and choose Table properties in the pop-up menu **(Figure 18.26)**. The Table Properties dialog box appears.

2. Check the Table width and/or Table min. height boxes to activate them **(Figure 18.27)**.

3. Enter the desired values in pixels or as a percentage of the browser window size.

4. Click OK to save the changes **(Figure 18.28)**.

✔ Tip

■ You can't make the table too small for its contents. If you try, Netscape will ignore you in the Editor window. Most browsers when viewing the table will expand it as necessary, regardless of the measurements you've specified, so that the entire contents can be seen.

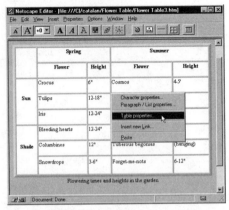

Figure 18.26 *Right click the table and choose Table properties in the pop-up menu.*

Figure 18.27 *Check the Table width box and enter the desired value in pixels, or as a percentage of the browser window's size.*

Figure 18.28 *The table occupies only 90% of the window now.*

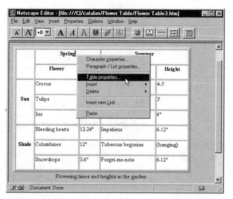

Figure 18.29 *Right click the desired cell and choose Table properties in the pop-up menu.*

Figure 18.30 *Enter the desired cell width in pixels, or as a percentage of the entire table size in the bottom section of the Cell tab.*

Figure 18.31 *The Spring cell is now better proportioned with respect to the rest of the table, although further adjustments probably wouldn't hurt.*

Changing a cell's height and width

You may wish to adjust the height and width of individual cells to make the table more attractive. Although browsers make an effort to size the elements accordingly, sometimes the results are wanting.

To change an individual cell's height and width:

1. Select the desired cell and choose Table in the Properties menu or right click the desired cell and choose Table properties in the pop-up menu **(Figure 18.29)**. The Table Properties dialog box appears.

2. In the Cell tab, check the Cell width and/or Cell min. height boxes to activate them **(Figure 18.30)**.

3. Enter the desired values in pixels or as a percentage of the total table size.

4. Click OK to save the changes **(Figure 18.31)**.

✔ Tip

■ You can't make a cell too small for its contents. Most browsers when viewing the table will expand each cell as necessary, regardless of the measurements you've specified, so that the entire contents can be seen. However, the contents may be divided into separate lines. To keep the entry all on one line, consult *Controlling line breaks in a cell* on page 225.

Changing a cell's height and width

Aligning a cell's contents

Different browsers may show the contents of the cells in a table in their own way, by default, which may or may not be how you think the data looks best. To gain a little more control over the alignment of a cell's contents, set the alignment for each cell individually or by row.

To align a cell's contents:

1. Click in the desired cell to select it and choose Table in the Properties menu and then click the Cell tab. Or right click the desired cell and choose Table properties in the pop-up menu **(Figure 18.32)**.

2. Select both a horizontal and vertical alignment in the Text alignment section **(Figure 18.33)**.

3. If desired, click Apply to see the changes and then adjust the options until you are satisfied.

4. Click OK to close the dialog box and save the changes **(Figure 18.34)**.

To align all the cells in a row:

1. Click in the desired row to select it.

2. Choose Table in the Properties menu and then click the Row tab.

3. Select both a horizontal and vertical alignment in the Text alignment section.

4. If desired, click Apply to see the changes.

5. Click OK to close the dialog box. All of the cells in the selected row will be aligned in the same way according to the options chosen in step 3.

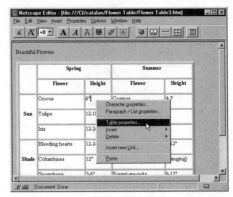

Figure 18.32 *Right click the desired cell and choose Table properties in the pop-up menu.*

Figure 18.33 *In the Cell tab, choose the desired alignment by clicking on the corresponding radio buttons under Horizontal and Vertical.*

Figure 18.34 *The cell's contents are aligned to the right in this example.*

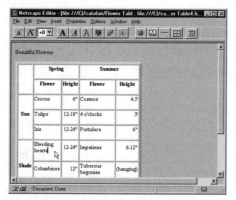

Figure 18.35 *Click in the cell whose contents you wish to appear on one line.*

Figure 18.36 *Uncheck the Wrap text box in the Text section of the Cell tab.*

Controlling line breaks in a cell

Unless you specify otherwise, browsers will divide the lines of text in a cell as it decides on the height and width of each column and row. With Netscape, you can set certain cells so that the contents are not divided.

To control the line breaks in a cell:

1. Click in the cell that should not be broken **(Figure 18.35)**.

2. Choose Table in the Properties menu and then click the Cell tab.

3. Uncheck the Wrap text option in the Text section **(Figure 18.36)**.

4. Click Apply to apply the changes or OK to close the dialog box and save the changes **(Figure 18.37)**.

Figure 18.37 *The table and cell widths are adjusted so that the cell's contents fit on a single line.*

Changing the color of a table, row, or cell

You can change the color of the entire table or just of an individual cell or row of cells to make important information stand out (or distract the user, as you prefer).

To change the color of a table, row, or cell:

1. Click anywhere in the table, row or cell to select it, choose Table in the Properties menu and then click the tab that corresponds to the part of the table you wish to modify: Table, Row, or Cell. Or right click the desired element and choose Table properties in the pop-up menu **(Figure 18.38)**.

2. Check the Table color, Row color, or Cell color option near the bottom of the dialog box **(Figure 18.39)**.

3. Click Choose Color. The Color dialog box appears.

4. Click on the desired color and click OK to close the dialog box.

5. Click Apply to see the changes right away. Make further changes and click Apply until you're satisfied with the results.

6. Click OK to close the dialog box and save the changes **(Figure 18.40)**.

✔ **Tips**

■ Not everyone has a color monitor. Be sure you choose colors that have a high enough contrast to be effective on grayscale monitors.

■ Right click the table, row, or cell and choose Table properties in the pop-up menu that appears to display the Table Properties dialog box.

Figure 18.38 *Right click the desired cell, row, or table and choose Table properties in the menu.*

Figure 18.39 *Click the appropriate tab (Table, Row, or Cell) and then mark the color option in the bottom part of the dialog box. Click Choose Color to select a new color.*

Figure 18.40 *The selected element's background color is changed.*

226

Advanced Page Design

Advanced is a relative term, of course. While the topics discussed in this chapter may be advanced for those new to Netscape Gold and to designing Web pages in general, seasoned HTML writers would be hard pressed to agree.

HTML, or Hypertext Markup Language, is the stuff that pages are made of. It looks a little bit like WordPerfect formatting in the early days of computers: to make something bold you had to add <B> in front of the word. On screen it looked terrible, but once printed, it *almost* made the tags worthwhile.

Netscape Gold is great for simple page design. It makes inserting images and adding special attributes to them (like alignment or size) very simple. It is much more careful about its end brackets than any human could ever be. However, it has certain limitations that can be overcome with a little manual editing.

For example, in Netscape Gold, you cannot apply logical formatting such as emphasis or strong. You cannot create forms or frames. And, Netscape inserts information about its own company on every page you create, which you may decide not to include.

If you'd like to learn more about HTML, you might try my other book: *HTML for the World Wide Web: Visual QuickStart Guide*, also published by Peachpit Press.

Standard HTML

In the fight between universality and features, Netscape stands squarely behind the latter. In fact, there are a certain set of HTML tags, known as *Netscape extensions* that used to only work with Netscape. Other browsers, such as Mosaic and Microsoft's Internet Explorer have been gradually accepting most, but not all, of these extensions. To see what kind of HTML code is produced by Netscape Gold, and how compatible it is with other browsers, consult *How Netscape Gold translates into HTML* on page 276.

When designing your page, you have to decide between standard HTML, which, by definition, can be viewed properly in all Web browsers, and Netscape's extensions, which may make your page more attractive—at least to those who can view it correctly. Generally, the answer is somewhere between there and here. The trick is to view your finished page from more than one browser so that you can see which effects are totally lost on non-Netscape browsers, and which information needs to be reworked.

One last solution is to create several versions of your pages, one that uses Netscape's extensions freely and another that presents the information in a way all browsers can understand—using standard HTML.

Figure 19.1 *Although you can create interesting effects with Netscape Gold, be aware that not all browsers view these elements in the same way.*

Figure 19.2 *Not surprisingly, Netscape's own browser displays the page exactly as it was in the Editor window.*

Figure 19.3 *The same page in Mosaic appears decidedly different. In particular, the font size and color information is lost, and the horizontal lines are full black instead of gray.*

Figure 19.4 *Click where you want to insert a nonbreaking space (or select a space you want to convert in a nonbreaking space as shown here).*

Figure 19.5 *Choose Nonbreaking Space in the Insert menu.*

Figure 19.6 *With nonbreaking spaces between each word, no matter how narrow the user makes the window, the line won't break.*

Figure 19.7 *In other browsers like Mosaic, the nonbreaking spaces are shown as regular ones.*

Adding nonbreaking spaces

HTML doesn't allow you to add extra spaces between words. Netscape's nonbreaking space not only lets you put more than one space between words, but it also holds those words together like glue. They can't be separated by a line break.

To add a nonbreaking space:

1. Click in the Editor window where you wish to enter the nonbreaking space **(Figure 19.4)**.

2. Choose Nonbreaking Space in the Insert menu **(Figure 19.5)**. The space is inserted **(Figure 19.6)**.

✔ Tips

■ You can also insert a nonbreaking space by pressing Shift+Space.

■ Many browsers do not recognize nonbreaking spaces. They will divide words and eliminate the spaces as always **(Figure 19.7)**.

Adding nonbreaking spaces

Adding HTML tags manually

Thankfully, you are not limited to the tags that Netscape can insert through its commands and buttons. You can add any HTML tag manually.

To add an HTML tag manually:

1. Place the cursor where you wish to insert the opening HTML tag **(Figure 19.8)**.

2. Choose HTML Tag in the Insert menu **(Figure 19.9)**. The Insert HTML Tag dialog box appears.

3. Type a single HTML tag in the text area **(Figure 19.10)**. Netscape automatically checks to see if you have typed an end bracket (>) and that you have enclosed all attributes in quotation marks.

4. If desired, click Verify to have Netscape check if your HTML tag is standard HTML. (This is something like asking the fox to guard your chickens. See page 228.)

5. Click OK to insert the tag. It appears as a big, yellow tag in the Editor window **(Figure 19.11)**.

6. If necessary, click where you wish to insert the closing HTML tag and repeat steps 2–5 **(Figure 19.12, Figure 19.13, and Figure 19.14)**.

7. Browse the page to view the effects of the HTML tag **(Figure 19.15)**.

Figure 19.8 *Click where you want to insert the HTML tag manually.*

Figure 19.9 *Choose HTML Tag in the Insert menu.*

Figure 19.10 *Type one single tag in the HTML Tag dialog box. Click OK to close the dialog box.*

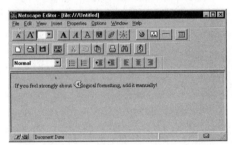

Figure 19.11 *The HTML Tag is shown with a big, yellow tag.*

Figure 19.12 *To insert the closing tag, click in the Editor window where you wish to put it.*

Figure 19.13 *Type the closing tag in the HTML Tag dialog box and click OK.*

Figure 19.14 *The closing tag looks just like the first. It's not pointed the other way.*

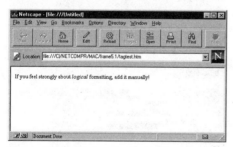

Figure 19.15 *The browser knows how to interpret the HTML tag correctly.*

✔ **Tips**

■ For a listing of exactly what Netscape can do on its own, consult *How Netscape Gold translates into HTML* on page 276.

■ If you want to add logical formatting, you'll have to do it manually. Netscape Gold only inserts physical formatting (bold, italic, etc.).

■ I wouldn't try adding forms or frames to your page with Netscape Gold. Besides the fact that the program has a hard time dealing with those features and bombs a lot, it's just not worth the hassle. Use a text editor.

■ You can only insert one tag at a time. For tags that have opening and closing versions, you'll have to insert the opening tag, type the affected text and then insert the closing tag.

Adding HTML tags manually

Editing HTML tags externally

You can look at the HTML tags on your page by opening the page with any text editor. Once in the text editor, you can remove Netscape's annoying, automatic self-identification tags and add features that Netscape Gold does not support.

To edit HTML tags externally:

1. From the Editor window, choose Edit Document Source in the View menu **(Figure 19.16)**. Netscape launches the program you've specified for editing HTML *(see page 233)* and opens the page **(Figure 19.17)**.

2. Make any desired changes.

3. Choose Save As in the File menu of the text editor **(Figure 19.18)**.

4. Choose Text Only for the format and give the file either the .htm or .html extension. Otherwise, browsers won't recognize the file **(Figure 19.19)**.

✔ Tips

■ Of course, you don't even have to open Netscape to edit your HTML tags manually. Simply open the text editor (Notepad or Wordpad will do fine, though you can use a fancier word processor if you prefer) and then open the HTML document.

■ When you choose Edit Document Source, Netscape launches a new instance of the text editor even if there's one already open. To reduce clutter, open the document manually.

■ If you use Microsoft Word, be sure to convert the page from Text Only (and not from HTML) when it opens. This way, you'll see the actual tags.

Figure 19.16 *With the page in the Editor window, choose Edit Document Source in the Edit menu.*

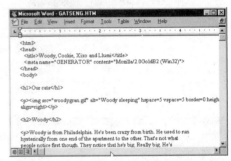

Figure 19.17 *The page is opened with the selected text editor. Now you can see and edit the HTML tags.*

Figure 19.18 *Choose Save As in the text editor's File menu.*

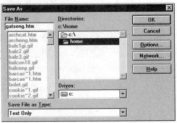

Figure 19.19 *Make sure you save the file in Text Only format with the .htm or .html extension.*

Figure 19.20 *Choose Editor Preferences in the Options menu.*

Figure 19.21 *Click Browse next to HTML source in the External editors section.*

Figure 19.22 *Find the text editor that you want to use and click Open.*

Figure 19.23 *The path to the text editor now appears in the HTML source text box.*

Specifying a program for editing HTML tags

Since HTML documents are always saved in Text Only or ASCII format, you can use virtually any word processor—from Word-Pad to WordPerfect—to edit HTML tags. You can specify which program you'd like to use, and Netscape will launch it automatically when you decide to edit the tags manually *(see page 232)*.

To specify a program for editing HTML tags:

1. Choose Editor Preferences in the Options menu **(Figure 19.20)**.

2. Click the General tab to see the general Editor preferences.

3. In the External editors section, click Browse next to HTML source **(Figure 19.21)**. The Open dialog box appears.

4. Locate the desired text editor on your hard disk and click Open **(Figure 19.22)**. The path to the program now appears next to HTML source in the Editor Preferences dialog box **(Figure 19.23)**.

5. Click OK to close the dialog box.

Specifying a program for editing HTML tags

Adding JavaScript to your page

Java is a unique language, developed by Sun Microsystems, that lets you add little applications to your pages. JavaScript is a special version of Java that runs with Netscape. There are entire books that explain how to program with Java. Here you'll learn how to insert the code into your page.

To add JavaScript to your page:

1. In the Editor window, type the code that you wish to insert and select it **(Figure 19.24)**.

2. Choose Character in the Properties menu and then JavaScript (Client) or JavaScript (Server) in the submenu **(Figure 19.25)**. JavaScript client text is shown in red, while JavaScript server text is shown in blue. Both are shown in fixed width text **(Figure 19.26)**.

3. Choose Browse Document to see the JavaScript code in action **(Fig. 19.27)**.

✔ Tips

■ You can also convert text into Java-Script code by selecting Text in the Properties menu, clicking the Character tab and selecting the desired Java-Script option.

■ For more information about Java and JavaScript, go to *http://home.netscape.com/eng/mozilla/3.0/handbook/javascript/ index.html*.

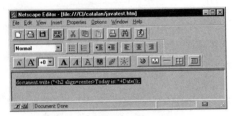

Figure 19.24 *Type your JavaScript code and then select it.*

Figure 19.25 *Choose Character in the Properties menu and then JavaScript (Client) or JavaScript (Server) in the submenu.*

Figure 19.26 *The JavaScript client text is shown in red in a fixed width font.*

Figure 19.27 *In the browser, the JavaScript is interpreted.*

Publishing a Page

Once you've finished designing your page, you have to make it accessible to your public. First you should test your page and make sure all your images appear as they should, that your text is formatted properly, and that your links lead where you intended.

Then you're ready to transfer the files to your server. Netscape Gold boasts a one-step publishing command that copies a page and its associated images to a given location on a remote server.

Once your page is up and running, you'll want to put out the word so that people know how to find it.

Testing your page

You should always test your Web pages in at least one browser, if not more. It is not necessary to connect to the server to test your pages. Instead, use the Open Local or Open File command to open the pages from your local computer.

To test your pages:

1. Make the browser active and choose Open File in Browser in the File menu **(Figure 20.1)**.

2. In the Open dialog box that appears, locate and select the file that you wish to test and click Open **(Figure 20.2)**. The page appears in the browser.

3. Go through the whole page and make sure it looks exactly the way you want it to **(Figure 20.3)**. For example:

Is the formatting what you wanted?

Does each of your links lead to the correct destination?

Are your images aligned properly?

Have you included your name and e-mail address (preferably in a link, and/or formatted with Address) so that your users can contact you with comments and suggestions?

4. Choose Edit Document in Netscape's File menu or click the Edit button on the toolbar to switch to editing mode **(Figure 20.4)**. The page appears in the Editor window **(Figure 20.5)**.

5. Make any necessary changes.

6. Choose Save in the File menu to save the changes **(Figure 20.6)**.

Figure 20.1 *Choose Open File in Browser in the File menu.*

Figure 20.2 *Choose the page on your hard disk that you wish to test.*

Figure 20.3 *Read the page over, checking for spelling and formatting errors. Do the images appear as desired? Do the links go where they should?*

Testing your page

Figure 20.4 *Choose Edit Document in the File menu.*

Figure 20.5 *In the Editor window, make any necessary corrections.*

Figure 20.6 *Choose Save in the File menu to save the corrections made to your Web page.*

7. Choose Browse Document in the File menu or click the View in Browser icon to view the changes.

8. Repeat steps 1–5 until you are satisfied with your pages. Don't get discouraged if it takes several tries.

9. View your page with other browsers to make sure your page will be attractive no matter what browser your readers use.

10. Transfer the files to the server, if you haven't done so already *(see page 238)*.

11. Test all your links again to make sure that they work correctly from the server.

✔ Tips

■ Use several browsers (Mosaic, Lynx, Microsoft Internet Explorer, etc.) to test your pages. You never know what browser your user is going to view your pages with.

■ You can test the links locally by clicking them as long as the destination documents are in the same relative position on your computer. In other words, if the files will be in the same directory on the server, they should be in the same directory on your hard disk.

Testing your page

Publishing your page

Netscape Gold has a special publishing option that automatically transfers all of the files in your Web site to your server so that your public has access to them.

To publish your page:

1. Open a connection to the Internet if you're not already connected.

2. Choose Publish in the File menu **(Figure 20.7)**. The Publish Files dialog box appears.

3. If you are publishing one page (with its images), next to Include files check Images in the document. If you are publishing more than one page, next to Include files check All files in document's folder **(Figure 20.8)**.

4. The images from the current document (or all the images in the current page's folder) appear in the scroll list. Click the files that you want to copy to the server, using the Select None and Select All buttons as necessary. Your readers will only be able to see the images on a page if you copy them to the server.

5. Enter the location on the server where the files should be copied **(Fig. 20.9)**. If you're not sure what to type here, ask your Internet service provider. Typically, it will be the FTP address of your Web site on the server.

6. Enter your user name and password. If desired, click Save password so that you don't have to enter it each time you publish a page.

Figure 20.7 *With the Editor window active, choose Publish in the File menu.*

Figure 20.8 *In the Local files section, choose the files you wish to copy to the server.*

Figure 20.9 *In the Publishing Location area, enter the FTP or Web address where you wish to publish your page. Enter a name and password if necessary.*

Figure 20.10 *As the files are published, a dialog box gives you a progress report.*

Figure 20.11 *An alert appears when Netscape has finished publishing your files.*

7. Click OK to send the files to the server. As the selected HTML page and the additional files listed in the scroll box are copied, a dialog box keeps you apprised of the progress **(Figure 20.10)**. An alert assures you that you have successfully published the page **(Figure 20.11)**.

✔ Tips

■ The default publishing location on the server should appear in the pop-up menu. However, you can type any location that you wish. The addresses that you use will be recorded, and you can choose them from the pop-up menu during future publishing sessions. You can always go back to the default location by clicking Use Default Location. For more information, consult *Setting up a default publishing location* on page 240.

■ The name of the file you are about to publish appears at the top of the Publish Files dialog box. If this is not the file you want to publish, click Cancel and start again. The page to be published is always the one active in the Editor window when you chose Publish in the File menu.

■ If you are wary of automatic gadgets, you can publish your pages manually with FTP. For more information, consult *Uploading a file with FTP* on page 51.

Publishing your page

Setting up a default publishing location

Generally, one always publishes to the same location on the server. You can define that location so that you don't have to enter it manually during each publishing session.

To set up a default publishing location:

1. Choose Editor Preferences in the Options menu **(Figure 20.12)**.

2. Click the Publish tab to see the Publish preferences.

3. In the Default publishing location section, enter an FTP or Web address where you want to publish your pages **(Figure 20.13)**. If you're not sure what address to use, contact your Internet service provider.

4. If desired, enter your user name and password at the bottom of the dialog box. Click Save password so that Netscape doesn't ask you for your password each time you publish a page.

5. Click OK to save the changes.

✔ Tip

■ If you don't enter your user name and password in the Editor Preferences dialog box, Netscape will ask you for it when you publish your page. If you *do* enter it, anyone with access to your computer will be able to publish files to your FTP or Web site.

Figure 20.12 *Choose Editor Preferences in the Options menu.*

Figure 20.13 *Enter the location where you publish most of your pages in the Publish to text box. If desired, enter a user name and password.*

Figure 20.14 *Choose Default Publish Location in the Go menu.*

Figure 20.15 *Click Yes to enter the default location.*

Figure 20.16 *Enter your Web site's home page, or other page that you view regularly, in the Browse to text box.*

Figure 20.17 *The desired page on the server is shown in the browser.*

Viewing your published page

Once you've published your page, you should connect to your server and check that it looks the way it's supposed to.

To view your published page:

1. Open your connection to the Internet, if it isn't already.

2. Choose Default Publishing Location in the Go menu **(Figure 20.14)**.

3. If you haven't yet entered the location of your Web page, you can do that now. Click Yes in the alert box **(Figure 20.15)**.

4. In the Editor Preferences dialog box that appears, type the URL of the page you would like to view in the Browse to text box **(Figure 20.16)**. Click OK to close the dialog box.

5. Your published page is shown in the browser **(Figure 20.17)**. Notice the URL in the Location field; it is *not* local.

✔ Tips

■ A good choice for the Browse to text box is your Web site's home page. That way you can quickly jump to your own base and test all of your published pages.

■ You can always get back to the Editor Preferences dialog box by choosing Editor Preferences in the Options dialog box, and then clicking the Publish tab *(see page 256)*.

Viewing your published page

Advertising your site

With the growing popularity of the Web, there has come an explosion in services for both Web page publishers (that's you!) and browsers. There are many ways to get the word out about your page. Here are some starters.

To advertise your site:

1. Use the What's New fill in forms at free Web indexing services like Yahoo! **(Fig. 20.18)**, NCSA Mosaic, and Global Network Navigator **(Fig. 20.19)**.

Yahoo!: *http://add.yahoo.com/bin/add?*

NCSA Mosaic: *http://www.ncsa.uiuc.edu/SDG/Software/Mosaic/Docs/whats-new-form.html*

Global Network Navigator: *http://gnn.com/gnn/netizens/addform.html*

(There are no spaces in any of these URLs. The hyphens are *not* optional.)

2. Pay a company to advertise your page for you.

3. Post a note in the moderated newsgroup *comp.infosystems.www.announce* or the unmoderated *comp.internet.net-happenings* or in newsgroups that have similar interests as your Web site.

4. Send e-mail to your associates and friends. You can include the URL for your site in all your correspondence with a signature *(see page 130).*

5. Send e-mail to the creators of other sites with similar interests or topics.

Figure 20.18 *Fill in Yahoo's form to add your page to their index.*

Figure 20.19 *Global Network's Netizens directory is especially designed for personal home pages.*

Part III:
Preferences

Personalizing Netscape Navigator

21

Figure 21.1 *Choose General Preferences in the Options menu to view the General Preferences dialog box.*

The settings in the General Preferences dialog box control a variety of features, from the fonts you view pages in to colors, helper applications, and language. To access the General Preferences box, choose General Preferences in the Options menu **(Figure 21.1)**.

The General Preferences dialog box is divided into seven sections called *tabs*. Click a tab's name to make it active and access its settings. Each tab is described in detail in the following pages.

Once you've made the desired changes to the settings, click OK to save the changes, or Cancel to leave the dialog box without saving them. Click Help to access Netscape's Help file.

General Preferences

Appearance

Click the Appearance tab in the General Preferences dialog box to display the Appearance preferences. Use the Appearance preferences to control the appearance of the toolbar, the initial window (and page) that Netscape shows upon launch, and links.

Toolbars ——

Startup ——

Link Styles ——

Appearance (side tab)

Toolbars

Choose Pictures to see smaller representations of the toolbar buttons.

Choose Text to see only the words on the buttons.

Choose Pictures and Text to see both.

Startup
Click Netscape Browser so that the first window you see when entering Netscape is the Web Browser. Click Netscape Mail to start with the Mail window (and automatically check your mail). Click Netscape News to start with the News window.

If you've chosen Netscape Browser under On Startup Launch above, choose Blank page to open Netscape with a clean, blank window (*see page 17*).

Choose Home Page Location and type a URL address to have Netscape open a particular page upon launch (*see page 17*).

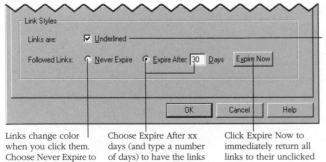

Link Styles
Click Underlined to display the hypertext links in your Web pages with an underline (*see page 25*). Uncheck it to hide the line.

Links change color when you click them. Choose Never Expire to keep the "visited" color forever.

Choose Expire After xx days (and type a number of days) to have the links return to their original color after a certain number of days.

Click Expire Now to immediately return all links to their unclicked color.

Fonts

Click the Fonts tab in the General Preferences dialog box to display the Fonts preferences. Use the Fonts preferences to choose the default font encoding for the documents you browse, as well as the particular fonts that should be used.

Encoding ——

Choose fonts ——

Encoding

Choose an encoding that matches the alphabet of the documents you will read. An encoding describes the relationship between characters and their hexadecimal representations.

Choose Fonts

Click one of the Choose Font buttons to designate the desired fonts.

Most of the text you see in a document will be displayed with a proportional font like Times or Helvetica.

The text displayed in entry forms and sometimes in block quotes or other special parts of a page is displayed with a fixed font like Courier.

When you click the Choose Font button, you'll see this dialog box. Select a font and a font size and then click OK to save the changes.

Fonts

Colors

You have some control over the colors used on the pages you browse. You can choose a different color for new and visited links and for regular text. For the background, choose either a color or an image. Finally, you can make these choices override the options used in any individual Web page.

Links and Text ———

Background ———

Override ———

Links and Text
You can choose your own colors for links you haven't visited (Links), links you have visited (Followed Links) and for regular text (Text). Simply click Custom and then click Choose Color. Choose a color in the dialog box that appears and click OK. The new color will be shown in the swatch.

To change a color, first click the Custom button.

The current color is shown in the swatch.

After clicking Custom, click the Choose Color button.

Background
You may choose a special color or even an image for the background of all the pages you browse.

To choose a background color, click Custom and then click Choose Color.

To choose an image, click Image file, then click Browse and locate the desired file (GIF or JPEG format) on your hard disk.

Override
Some Web page designers define their own colors for text, links, and background. You can choose to override their choices.

Click Always Use My Colors, Overriding Document if you want your colors (chosen above) to take precedence over a particular Web page designer's fancy. For example, if you're having trouble reading a page because the Web designer chose rotten colors, you can go back to normal colors by using this option.

Images

Click the Images tab in the General Preferences dialog box to display the Images preferences. You can choose the method in which extra colors should be displayed and how images should be loaded onto the page.

Choosing Colors

Display images

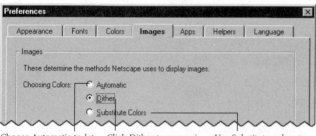

Choose Automatic to let Netscape decide how to best deal with the colors.

Click Dither to approximate the image's colors by using a combination of the available ones. Dithering gives the best results but may be slow.

Use Substitute colors to use the existing colors in place of missing ones. Substitute is faster but gives poorer results.

Choosing Colors

Many monitors can only view 256 colors at once. If you try to load several images that contain more than the allowed number of colors, Netscape has to fudge the results: either by dithering or substituting colors.

Choose While Loading if you want to see the images as they load.

Choose After Loading to display the images all at once, after all the data has been received. On a fast network, this may be slightly faster.

Display images

If you have chosen Auto Load Images in the Options menu, Netscape will load images as it loads each page. With the preferences in this section, you can choose to display the images incrementally while loading, or display them all at once, when all the information has been received.

Images

Apps

Click the Apps tab in the General Preferences dialog box to see the application preferences for the programs you use in conjunction with Netscape. You can also choose the program that you wish to use to view HTML tags *(see page 232)* and the folder where temporary files should be stored.

Telnet applications
View Source
Temporary Directory

Click Browse and locate the Telnet application that you wish to use. Telnetting means connecting to a remote computer as if you were there in person.

A TN3270 application is for telnetting to an IBM mainframe. Click Browse to locate the desired TN3270 application on your hard disk.

Telnet applications
You can designate a Telnet or TN3270 application of your choice for connecting to another computer via Telnet through Netscape.

Click Browse to locate the desired program with which to view a page's HTML tags, when you select Document Source in the View menu. For example, you might choose to view HTML tags with Microsoft Word or Word Perfect.

View Source
You can designate which program to launch when viewing HTML tags.

Type the path of the directory where temporary files should be stored.

Temporary directory
When Netscape encounters a file it cannot display by itself, it downloads the file and launches a helper application to deal with it. Once the file has been viewed, it is deleted. You can choose where these temporary files should be kept on your hard disk.

Apps

Helpers

Click the Helpers tab in the General Preferences dialog box to see the Helpers preferences. You can choose which helper applications should be launched according to which files Netscape encounters out on the Web, or if the files should simply be saved.

List of file types

File type

Action

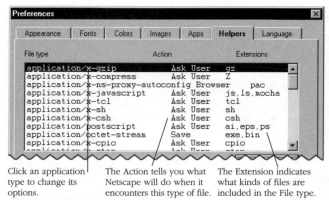

Click an application type to change its options.

The Action tells you what Netscape will do when it encounters this type of file.

The Extension indicates what kinds of files are included in the File type.

List of file types

Many different kinds of files are listed, along with the action that will take place when Netscape encounters them, and the extensions that define those kinds of files.

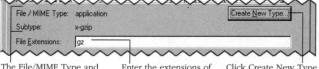

The File/MIME Type and Subtype give the same information as in the scroll list above, for the selected type.

Enter the extensions of the files that you wish to define as the selected File type.

Click Create New Type to define a file type for a kind of file not already in the list.

File type

This section defines the file type, lets you choose a new file type, and lets you see (or add) new extensions.

Click View in Browser to view the file in Netscape, if possible.

Choose Save to Disk to have Netscape automatically save the files with this extension to your hard disk.

Click Unknown: Prompt User to have Netscape ask you what to do when it encounters a file type that it doesn't recognize.

Action

You tell Netscape what you want it to do with each kind of file it finds. You can view the file directly (if Netscape can), save it, have it ask you, or launch a helper application that, in turn, opens the file.

Choose Launch the Application (and click Browse and find the application on your hard disk) to have Netscape automatically open a program that can open the files that have this extension.

Helpers

Language

Click the Language tab in the General Preferences dialog box to see the language preferences. When a page on the Web is available in more than one language, you can tell the server what language(s) you prefer to browse by creating an "accept list" of languages.

Accept
Language ─

Accept Language

You can create a priority list of languages in which you prefer files to be downloaded or viewed through the Accept list. Then Netscape advises the server of the desired languages and if the server understands, it gives you access to the appropriate language version.

If the desired language or region does not appear in the left list, enter the non-standard language or region and then click the down arrow to add it to the accept list. The first tag should be a two letter ISSO 639 language abbreviation. The second two letters should be an ISO 3166 country tag.

Click a Language/ Region in the left list to select it.

Click the right pointing arrow to add the new language to the accept list. Click the left pointing arrow to remove a language from the Accept list.

The acceptable languages are listed in the right list in order of preference.

Editor Preferences

Options

Figure 22.1 *Choose Editor Preferences in Netscape Gold's Options menu.*

The settings in the Editor Preferences dialog box control how documents are created, what colors they use and how they're published. To access the Editor Preferences box, choose Editor Preferences in the Options menu **(Figure 22.1)**. The Editor Preferences are only available in Netscape Gold.

The Editor Preferences dialog box is divided into three sections called *tabs*. Click a tab's name to make it active and access its settings. Each tab is described in detail in the following pages.

Once you've made the desired changes to the settings, click OK to save the changes, or Cancel to leave the dialog box without saving them. Click Help to access Netscape Gold's Help file.

General

Click the General tab to change the default author's name, to choose external text and image editors, and to specify which pages you would like to use as a template when creating new Web pages of your own.

Author name —
External editors —
New document template —
Autosave —

Author name

The Author name identifies the pages you create. The information does not appear on the Web page when viewed with a browser, but instead is inserted into the HTML tags and can be used by search services.

Type the name with which you wish to identify all the pages you create.

External editors

Netscape gives you a shortcut to the programs you use most often for editing HTML tags and images.

Type the path to a text editor that you would like to use, in addition to Netscape Gold, for viewing and modifying HTML tags. Or click Browse and locate the program on your hard disk.

Type the path to an image editor (like PaintShop Pro or Photoshop) that you would like to use for editing images. Or click Browse and locate the program on your hard disk.

New document template

When you choose New Document in the File menu and then From Template in the submenu, Netscape loads the page specified at left. You can create your own templates and type the path to them here.

Click Restore Default to use Netscape's default templates (at Netscape's Web site).

Autosave

Enter a number in the Automatically save document every xx minutes text box to have Netscape save your file periodically as you work.

General

Appearance

Click the Appearance tab to change the colors and background of the Web pages you create. The options chosen here don't affect the current page. To change the colors or background of the current page, choose Document in the Properties menu and click the Appearance tab (which looks just like this one).

Color schemes —
Custom colors —
Background image —

Netscape has designed a collection of color schemes that are different from the norm, but sill readable. Click in the pop-up menu to choose one.

Custom colors vs. Browser's colors and Color schemes
Click Use custom colors to use the options specified in the rest of this dialog box. Choose Use Browser's colors to use the colors specified in the Colors tab of the General Preferences dialog box.

Click the element whose color you wish to change. In the Color dialog box that appears, choose the desired color and click OK. The new color will be shown next to the corresponding element type.

Custom colors
Choose which color to use for regular text, new links (Link Text), links being clicked on (Active Link Text) and visited links (Followed Link Text).

Click Image file and then Browse for File to locate the desired image on your hard disk. If the image is smaller than the page, it will be tiled (repeated) to fit.

Background image
Choose an image, if desired, for the background of your Web pages.

255

Publish

Click the Publish tab to determine how
Netscape treats links and images in the
pages you create and edit, and to specify
the location of the server where you
wish your page and its associated
images to be copied when you choose
Publish in the File menu.

Links and images

**Default publish-
ing location**

Links and images

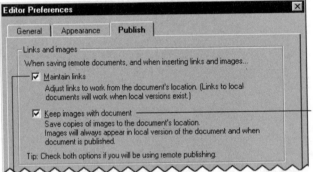

Check Keep images with document if
you want Netscape to copy all the
images inserted on a page to the
same directory on your hard disk that
contains the Web page itself.

Choose Maintain Links to have Netscape convert absolute links into relative
ones on the pages that you copy from the Web. This will enable the links to
continue to work correctly when you open them locally (from your hard disk).

Default publishing location
Specify where your pages should
be published when you choose
Publish in the File menu.

Type a URL in the Browse to
(HTTP) text box to determine
where the Default Publish Location
command in the Go menu takes
you (see page 241).

In the Publish to (FTP or HTTP) text
box, type the URL of the FTP or Web
site where you wish to publish your
files. If you're not sure, ask your
Internet service provider.

Enter your user name and password in the corresponding
boxes and click Save password so that Netscape doesn't ask
you for it each time. Of course, this lets anyone with access to
your computer publish documents to your FTP site. If you prefer, enter just the user name and let Netscape ask you for your
password manually.

Publish

Mail and News Prefs

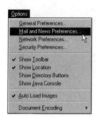

Figure 23.1 *Choose Mail and News Preferences in the Options menu to see the Mail and News Preferences dialog box.*

The settings in the Mail and News Preferences dialog box control many different aspects of the mail and news windows. To access the Mail and News Preferences dialog box, choose Mail and News Preferences in the Options menu **(Figure 23.1)**.

The Mail and News Preferences dialog box is divided into five sections called *tabs*. Click a tab's name to make it active and access its settings. Each tab is described in detail in the following pages.

Once you've made the desired changes to the settings, click OK to save the changes, or Cancel to leave the dialog box without saving them. Click Help to access Netscape's Help file.

Appearance

Click the Appearance tab in the Mail and
News Preferences dialog box to change
the way messages appear in the Mail
and News windows. You can choose the
font that messages should be displayed
in, as well as the style and size of quoted
sections. In addition, you can choose
not to use Netscape Mail at all!

Message Font —
**Styles for
quoted text** —
**Mail and
News Program** —
Pane Layout —

Message Font
In the General Preferences box *(see
page 246),* you chose a specific font
for proportional text and another
for fixed font text. Here, you can
choose which of those fonts should
be used for displaying messages in
the Mail and News windows.
(Unfortunately, the Message Composition window is not affected.)

Click Fixed Width Font to use the font
defined next to "Use the Fixed Font"
in the Fonts section of the General
Preferences dialog box.

Click Variable Width Font to use the
font defined next to "Use the Proportional Font" in the Fonts section of the
General Preferences dialog box.

Styles for quoted text
Many messages contain text from
earlier correspondence. You can
format that text with a special style
and size to set it apart from the current message's contents.

Click Plain, Bold, Italic or Bold Italic
to format quoted text with the corresponding style.

Click Plain to keep the quoted text at
the same size as regular text. Choose
Bigger or Smaller to change the size of
quoted text.

Mail program
If you already use Microsoft's
Exchange Client for e-mail with
Windows 95, you can continue to
do so, while using Netscape just for
browsing.

Click Use Netscape for Mail and News
to use Netscape for all mail and news
operations. This is the default option.

Click Use Exchange Client for Mail and
News to use Microsoft's software for
Mail and News. (Windows 95, only.)

Pane Layout
You can choose to display the
panes in the Mail and News windows in one of three ways: horizontally, vertically or stacked. For
an example of each, see page 91.

Composition

Click the Composition tab in the Mail and News Preferences dialog box to choose a bit format for your messages, whether or not to e-mail or save a copy of them, and if Netscape should automatically quote the original message when you compose its reply.

Format ——

Saving outgoing messages ——

Automatic Quoting ——

Format

Most e-mail servers in the US and Europe use 8 bit messages. If you are receiving messages from a MIME mail reader, you can change the setting to see the characters correctly.

Click Allow 8-bit for widest compatibility with e-mail servers in the US and Europe.

Click Mime Compliant to make Netscape interpret messages from MIME mail readers correctly.

Saving outgoing messages

Incoming mail messages are automatically saved to your hard disk. Outgoing e-mail and news messages are not. Use these options to save these messages automatically.

Type an e-mail address in Mail Messages or News Messages to send a copy of all outgoing messages to that address.

Enter a path on your hard disk in Mail File or News File to save a copy of all outgoing messages to your hard disk.

Automatic Quoting

When you reply to an e-mail message or news posting, it's often a good idea to remind the recipient what they were talking about by quoting their original message. You can have Netscape quote messages all the time (using this option) or just sometimes (see page 122).

Mark the Automatically quote original message when replying checkbox to have Netscape automatically quote the original message in the Message Composition window when you select Reply or Reply to All in the Message menu.

Composition

Servers

Click the Servers tab in the Mail and News Preferences dialog box to enter information about the server name, your name, where mail should be stored, how large messages can be, whether they should be left on the server, and if Netscape should check for mail automatically.

Mail Server Data

Miscellaneous Mail

Miscellaneous News

Mail Server Data

You won't be able to send or receive mail until you fill in this important data. If you are not sure what to put in, ask your Service Provider.

The name of your Mail Server goes here.

Type the name of your Outgoing Mail Server here.

Type your user name here. This is the part of your e-mail address before the © symbol.

Miscellaneous Mail

Choose where to store mail messages on your hard disk, their maximum size, whether or not to remove them from the server, and if Netscape should check for mail automatically.

Enter the path to the directory on your hard disk where mail messages should be stored.

You can limit Mail messages to a certain size by typing a number for Size. Otherwise, click None.

Netscape automatically copies incoming mail to your hard disk. Choose whether to leave a copy on the server as well.

Have Netscape check for mail automatically by clicking Every and entering a number of minutes. Otherwise, click Never.

Miscellaneous News

In this area, you enter the name of your news server (ask your Service Provider), the directory where your newsgroup settings (News RC) should be stored, and how many messages you want to retrieve at a time.

Enter the name of your news server here. Ask your Service Provider if you're not sure.

Enter the path to the directory on your hard disk where the News RC file should be stored. The News RC file contains information about which newsgroups you've subscribed to, among other things.

Choose how many news messages should be loaded from a newsgroup at once. The default is 100.

Servers

Identity

Click the Identity tab in the Mail and
News Preferences box to enter information about yourself, including your
name, e-mail address, the e-mail address
where you want to receive replies, and
the name of your organization. You can
also specify a signature file that will be
appended to every outgoing message.

Personal
information

Signature File

Personal information
All of the information you type here
appears on each message you send
out.

Type your name as you wish it to
appear on every outgoing message.

Type your e-mail address.

Type the address where you
want replies to be sent.

Type the name of your organization. If you don't type anything here, Netscape will use the name of your Service Provider automatically in all outgoing correspondence.

Signature File
You can create a text file and then
have Netscape automatically add it
the end of each message you send.
Most signatures include the writer's
name, e-mail address, sometimes
their snail-mail address, and a cute
quote. The only requirement is that
it be saved in Text Only format.

Click Browse to locate your signature file (any text file) on
the hard disk. For more information on signatures, consult
Creating a signature file on page 129.

Identity

Organization

Click the Organization tab in the Mail and News preferences dialog box to set certain defaults for the Mail and News windows. You can have Netscape remember your password, and automatically thread and sort messages as desired.

General —

Sort —

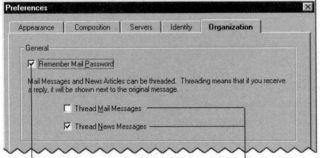

General
You'll need to let Netscape remember your password if you want it to check your mail automatically every few minutes. Threading your messages shows replies under the original message, slightly indented.

Click Remember Mail Password so that Netscape doesn't ask you to enter the password each time you check your mail. You must check this box if you want Netscape to check your mail automatically.

You can choose to thread mail or news messages by default. For more information, consult *Threading messages* on page 105.

Sort
You can choose default settings for the order in which Netscape sorts both Mail and News messages.

Click Date to order mail messages by date, Subject to order them by subject, and yes, Sender to order them by Sender, by default, each time you open the Mail window.

Click Date to order news postings by date, Subject to order them by subject, and yes, Sender to order them by Sender, by default, each time you open the News window.

For more information on sorting mail and news messages, consult *Putting your messages in order* on page 102.

Organization

Network Preferences

Figure 24.1 *Choose Network Preferences in the Options menu to view the Network Preferences dialog box.*

The settings in the Network Preferences dialog box control how Netscape works over a network. To view the Network Preferences dialog box, choose Network Preferences in the Options menu **(Figure 24.1)**.

The Network Preferences dialog box has three tabs. Click a tab's title to make it active and access its settings. Each tab is described in detail on the following pages.

Once you've made the desired changes to the settings, click OK to save the changes. Click Cancel to close the dialog box without saving changes. Click Help to access the Netscape Help file.

Network Preferences

Cache

Click the Cache tab in the Network Preferences dialog box to change the settings for the Disk and Memory caches, to change the directory, and to decide how often Netscape should compare a page saved in Cache with the actual page on the server.

Memory and Disk Caches

Disk Cache Directory

Verify Document

SSL Caching

Memory and Disk Caches

Netscape saves as many of the pages and images that you browse in its Memory and Disk Caches. Once a page or image is stored in a cache, it takes much less time to display. Netscape organizes the Cache when you exit the program. If it seems to take too long, try reducing the size of the Disk Cache.

Type a number in the text boxes to set the size of the Memory (RAM) or Disk (storage) caches. The defaults are shown here.

Click the Clear Memory Cache Now to make the specified amount of RAM available to other programs. The Memory Cache is automatically erased each time you close Netscape.

Click Clear Disk Cache Now to erase all the pages and images in the disk cache and make more space available on your hard disk.

Disk Cache Directory

You can choose where to store the disk cache on your hard disk.

Type the path to the directory where you want the disk cache to store the pages and images that you browse.

Verify Document

Pages on the Web are incredibly dynamic. Think of all the pages you've seen "under construction." You can have Netscape compare the document you have saved in cache with the current version once each time you open Netscape, every time you look at the page, or never.

Click Once per Session to have Netscape compare the cached version with the real page on the server only the first time you access the page during a session with Netscape.

Click Every Time to make Netscape compare the cached version with the server each time you browse the page.

Click Never to have Netscape always use the cached version without checking for changes.

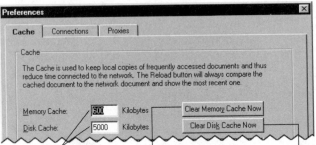

SSL Caching

Check this option to allow caching of SSL documents on your hard disk.

Connections

Click the Connections tab in the Network preferences dialog box to define the number of connections that Netscape can make at one time, and to set the size of the network buffer.

Number of Connections

Network Buffer Size

Type a number in the text box to determine how many connections Netscape should make at a time. The default is 4.

Number of Connections

The text and images on a page are distinct files on the server. Netscape can open more than one connection to the server in order to load the page more quickly, although the speed of each individual connection may deteriorate as a result.

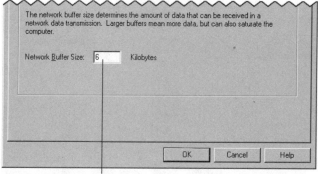

Type a number in the text box to define the size of the network buffer. The default for Windows is 32K.

Network Buffer Size

The size of the network buffer determines the amount of data that can be received at a time. A larger number means more information can be received, but may saturate the computer.

Connections

Proxies

Click the Proxies tab in the Network preferences dialog box to change how Netscape interacts with proxy software. In situations where a firewall protects internal computer networks from external access, Netscape needs proxy software to get by the firewall to remote servers without compromising security.

No Proxies

Manual Proxy Configuration

Automatic Proxy Configuration

Click No Proxies if you have a direct connection to the Internet.

No Proxies

If your computer is not on a network and/or if you have a direct Internet connection, you don't have to worry about proxies at all, and should choose No Proxies.

Click Manual Proxy Configuration and then click View to set or change each server's connection by typing its URL.

Manual Proxy Configuration

You can customize your own proxy configuration.

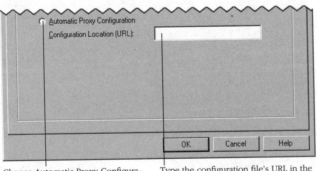

Automatic Proxy Configuration

You can also set Netscape up to take advantage of an already constructed configuration file.

Choose Automatic Proxy Configuration if you have already set up a configuration file for connecting to different servers.

Type the configuration file's URL in the text box so that Netscape can find it.

Proxies

Protocols

Click the Protocols tab in the Network preferences dialog box to determine when Netscape should alert you about accepting information from a server or when submitting a form via e-mail. You can also determine if your e-mail address should be sent as a password when connecting to anonymous FTP sites.

Alerts —

Anonymous FTP

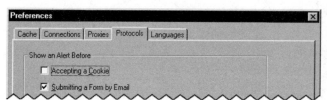

Alerts

Check either option to have Netscape present you with an alert before the corresponding information is received or sent.

Anonymous FTP

Check this option to have Netscape automatically send your e-mail address as a password (an Internet convention) when connecting to an anonymous FTP site. If you do not check this box, you may not be able to connect to some sites.

Protocols

Languages

Click the Languages tab in the Network preferences dialog box to enable Java and JavaScript.

Java/
JavaScript

Java/JavaScript
Check Enable Java if you want to be able to execute Java applets. Check Enable JavaScript to be able to interpret JavaScript code that has been embedded in a page's HTML code. Although enabling both options may not be 100% secure, some pages will not display properly without them.

Languages

Security Preferences

Figure 25.1 *Choose Security Preferences in the Options menu to view the Security Preferences dialog box.*

The settings in the Security Preferences dialog box help you protect your network, computer, or data. To access the dialog box, choose Security Preferences in the Options menu **(Figure 25.1)**.

The Security Preferences dialog box is divided into two sections called *tabs*. Click a tab's name to make it active and access its settings. Each tab is described in detail on the following pages.

Once you've made the desired changes to the security settings, click OK. Click Cancel to close the dialog box without saving the changes. Click Help to access the Netscape Help file.

Security Preferences

General

Click the General tab in the Security preferences dialog box to determine when Netscape should alert you about the security status of certain areas or documents and to configure SSL ciphers.

Show an Alert Before

SSL

Show an Alert Before
You can have Netscape alert you of possible security problems. The individual alert boxes contain a "Show this Alert Next Time" button which, when unchecked, gives the same result as checking one of the options in this dialog box.

SSL
Check each version of SSL to enable or disable it. Click Configure to choose which ciphers should be used for each version.

Passwords

Click the Passwords tab in the Security preferences dialog box to choose a password for Netscape and to determine when Netscape will ask you for it.

Set Password ——

Ask for
Password ——

Set Password

Click the Set Password to define a password that Netscape will use to protect your security certificates.

Ask for Password

Check one of the options under Ask for Password to determine how often Netscape will verify your password.

Passwords

Personal Certificates

Click the Personal Certificates tab in the Security preferences dialog box to see a list of your personal certificates, to get more information about them, to obtain new ones and eliminate obsolete ones and to determine which should be used by default.

Personal Certificates

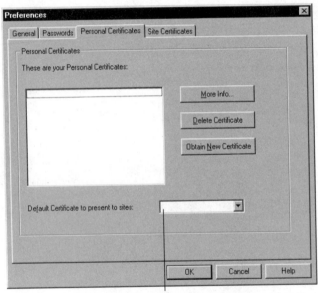

If you have more than one personal certificate, choose the one that you wish to use by default in the pop-up menu.

Personal Certificates

Personal certificates are your way of proving your identity when sending information through the Internet. For example, if you send an order with your credit card number, a personal certificate guarantees that the order came from you and not someone pretending to be you.

Netscape will list your current personal certificates in the scroll list. Select a certificate and click More Info to see what that particular certificate is for. Click Delete Certificate to eliminate the certificate. Click Obtain New Certificate (when you're on a valid Web page) to get a new personal certificate.

Site Certificates

Choose the Site Certificates tab in the Security preferences dialog box to change settings regarding site certificates. A site certificate indicates who operates the site, so that if you send information to them, you can be sure that they are who they say they are.

Site Certificates

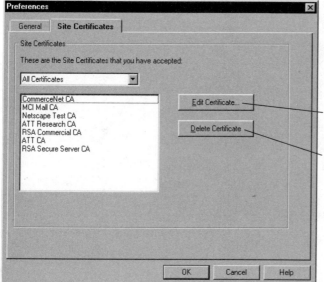

Site Certificates
You may receive various site certificates from companies that want to be able to securely identify themselves to you.

Click Edit Certificate to see the information in a site certificate and change its options.

Click Delete Certificate to eliminate the certificates that you no longer need.

Netscape Gold vs. HTML

Figure A.1 *Navigate to the page whose HTML codes you wish to view.*

Figure A.2 *Choose Document Source in the View menu.*

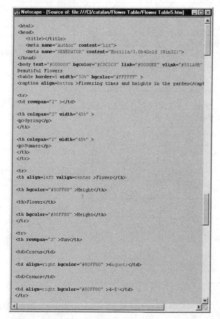

Figure A.3 *The HTML codes for the page are displayed in a new window.*

As you go about designing your page, you may want to know how Netscape converts the page's elements and formatting into HTML. If you are familiar with HTML, this information may help you determine how other browsers will display your page.

Viewing a page's HTML

One way to see how Netscape converts its pages into HTML is to look at your own. Or perhaps you want to study someone else's page and see how they achieved a particular effect.

To view a page's HTML:

1. Navigate to or open the page in Netscape's browser **(Figure A.1)**.

2. Choose Document Source in the View menu **(Figure A.2)**. Netscape opens a window and displays the HTML that makes up the current page **(Figure A.3)**.

✓ Tips

- Although no menus are available in the Document Source window, you can select what you want and copy it (Ctrl-C) as usual.

- You can see the HTML for a frame by selecting the frame and choosing Frame Source in the View menu.

- If you wish to edit the HTML code directly, first choose an HTML editor *(see page 254)* and then choose Edit Document Source in the Editor window's View menu.

How Netscape Gold translates into HTML

Use the following table to see how individual formatting commands in Netscape Gold are translated into HTML code. Note that most default values are not translated at all even if they have a command in Netscape. These cases are denoted in the table with a long hyphen (—). Only the HTML codes that Netscape can produce are listed here. For more information on inserting HTML codes not supported by Netscape Gold, consult *Adding HTML tags manually* on page 230.

How Netscape Gold translates into HTML

COMMAND NAME IN NETSCAPE GOLD	HTML CODE USED	COMPATIBILITY
Document Properties		
General		
Creation of page (automatic)	<html>	HTML 3.2
Header area (automatic)	<head>	HTML 3.2
Title	<title>	HTML 3.2
Author	<meta name="Author" content="xxx"	HTML 3.2
Description	<meta name="Description" content="xxx">	HTML 3.2
Generator (automatic)	<meta name="Generator" content="Mozilla/3Gold (Win 32)">	HTML 3.2
Keywords	<meta name="KeyWords" content="xxx">	HTML 3.2
Classification	<meta name="Classification" content="xxx">	HTML 3.2
Appearance		
Body area (automatic)	<body>	HTML 3.2
Normal text (color)	text="#rrggbb"	HTML 3.2*
Link Text (color)	link="#rrggbb"	HTML 3.2*
Active Link Text (color)	alink="#rrggbb"	HTML 3.2*
Followed Link Text (color)	vlink="rrggbb"	HTML 3.2*
Background Solid Color	bgcolor="rrggbb"	HTML 3.2*
Background Image file	background="image.gif"	HTML 3.2*
Character Styles		
Color		
Document's default color	—	
Custom color ▦	<font color="#rrggbb">	HTML 3.2*

*HTML Code used: n=any number (when describing width or height it can be either the number of pixels or a percentage of window size); #rrggbb=a color represented by giving the R, G, and B components in hexadecimals; indents indicate attributes that may be added, if desired, to the tag directly preceding it. Compatibility: HTML 3.2=part of standard HTML, up to version 3.2; *=not part of HTML 2 and probably not recognized by older browsers, N=Netscape only*

COMMAND NAME IN NETSCAPE GOLD	HTML CODE USED	COMPATIBILITY
Style		
Bold **A**	<b>	HTML 3.2
Italic *A*	<i>	HTML 3.2
Fixed width A	<tt>	HTML 3.2
Strikethrough	<strike>	HTML 3.2*
Superscript	<sup>	HTML 3.2
Subscript	<sub>	HTML 3.2
Blink	<blink>	N
Size		
A⁺, A⁻, or pop-up menu	<font size=n>	HTML 3.2*
JavaScript		
Client	<script>	N
Server	<server>	N
Paragraph Styles		
General		
Header 1, Header 2, etc.	<h1>, <h2>, *etc.*	HTML 3.2
Address	<address>	HTML 3.2
Formatted	<pre>	HTML 3.2
List item	<li>	HTML 3.2
Description Title	<dt>	HTML 3.2
Description Text	<dd>	HTML 3.2
Insert Indent	<ul>	HTML 3.2
Blockquote	<blockquote>	HTML 3.2
Align Left	—	
Align Right	<div align=right>	HTML 3.2*
Align Center	<center>	HTML 3.2
Lists		
Numbered List	<ol>	HTML 3.2
Number Style	type=	HTML 3.2*
Automatic	—	
1, 2, 3	—	
A, B, C	A	HTML 3.2*

*HTML Code used: n=any number (when describing width or height it can be either the number of pixels or a percentage of window size); #rrggbb=a color represented by giving the R, G, and B components in hexadecimals; indents indicate attributes that may be added, if desired, to the tag directly preceding it. Compatibility: HTML 3.2=part of standard HTML, up to version 3.2; *=not part of HTML 2 and probably not recognized by older browsers, N=Netscape only*

How Netscape Gold translates into HTML

COMMAND NAME IN NETSCAPE GOLD	HTML CODE USED	COMPATIBILITY
I, II, III	I	HTML 3.2*
a, b, c	a	HTML 3.2*
Starting Number	start=n	HTML 3.2*
Unnumbered (Bullet) List	<ul>	HTML 3.2
Bullet Style	type=	HTML 3.2*
Automatic	—	
Solid circle	disc	HTML 3.2*
Solid square	square	HTML 3.2*
Open square	circle *(really!)*	
Directory List	<dir>	outdated
Menu List	<menu>	outdated
Description List	<dl>	HTML 3.2
Links		
Link	<a href="url.#target">display text</a>	HTML 3.2
Target	<a name="targetname">targeted text</a>	HTML 3.2
Images		
Image	<img src="image.gif">	HTML 3.2
Alternative representations		
Image	lowsrc=	N
Text	alt=	HTML 3.2
Alignment		
	align=texttop	HTML 3.2*
	align=center	HTML 3.2*
	align=abscenter	HTML 3.2*
	—	
	align=bottom	HTML 3.2*

HTML Code used: n=any number (when describing width or height it can be either the number of pixels or a percentage of window size); #rrggbb=a color represented by giving the R, G, and B components in hexadecimals; indents indicate attributes that may be added, if desired, to the tag directly preceding it. Compatibility: HTML 3.2=part of standard HTML, up to version 3.2; *=not part of HTML 2 and probably not recognized by older browsers, N=Netscape only

COMMAND NAME IN NETSCAPE GOLD	HTML CODE USED	COMPATIBILITY
Text wrap		
	align=left	HTML 3.2*
	align=right	HTML 3.2*
Dimensions		
Height	height=	HTML 3.2*
Width	width=	HTML 3.2*
Space around image		
Left and right	hspace=	HTML 3.2*
Top and bottom	vspace=	HTML 3.2*
Solid border	border=	HTML 3.2*
Horizontal Lines		
Horizontal lines	\<hr\>	HTML 3.2
Height	*none if 2, otherwise,* size="n"	HTML 3.2*
Width	width="n" *or* width ="n%"	HTML 3.2*
Align	align=	HTML 3.2*
Left	left	
Center	—	HTML 3.2*
Right	right	HTML 3.2*
3d shading	*none when checked*, noshade *when unchecked*	HTML 3.2*
Tables		
General		
Table	\<table\>	HTML 3.2
Border line width	border=n	HTML 3.2*
Cell spacing	cellspacing=n	HTML 3.2*
Cell padding	cellpadding=n	HTML 3.2*
Table width	width="n" *or* width="n%"	HTML 3.2*
Table min. height	height="n" *or* height="n%"	HTML 3.2*
Table color	bgcolor="#rrggbb"	HTML 3.2*
Include caption	\<caption\>	HTML 3.2
above	—	
below table	align=bottom	HTML 3.2*

HTML Code used: n=any number (when describing width or height it can be either the number of pixels or a percentage of window size); #rrggbb=a color represented by giving the R, G, and B components in hexadecimals; indents indicate attributes that may be added, if desired, to the tag directly preceding it.
Compatibility: HTML 3.2=part of standard HTML, up to version 3.2; *=not part of HTML 2 and probably not recognized by older browsers, N=Netscape only

How Netscape Gold translates into HTML

How Netscape Gold translates into HTML

COMMAND NAME IN NETSCAPE GOLD	HTML CODE USED	COMPATIBILITY
Rows		
Table row	<tr>	HTML 3.2
Alignment—horizontal	align=	HTML 3.2
Left	left	HTML 3.2
Center	center	HTML 3.2
Right	right	HTML 3.2
Alignment—vertical	valign=	HTML 3.2*
Top	top	HTML 3.2*
Center	center	HTML 3.2*
Bottom	bottom	HTML 3.2*
Baselines	baseline *(no s)*	HTML 3.2*
Row color	bgcolor="#rrggbb"	HTML 3.2*
Cells		
Cell (automatic)	<td>	HTML 3.2
Header style	<th> *(instead of <td>)*	HTML 3.2
Cell spans		
rows	rowspan="n"	HTML 3.2
columns	colspan="n"	HTML 3.2
Alignment	*(see Rows above)*	
Wrap text	*nothing if checked;* nowrap *if not checked.*	HTML 3.2*
Cell width	width="n" *or* width="n%"	HTML 3.2*
Cell min. height	height="n" *or* height="n%"	HTML 3.2*
Cell color	bgcolor="#rrggbb"	HTML 3.2*

HTML Code used: n=any number (when describing width or height it can be either the number of pixels or a percentage of window size); #rrggbb=a color represented by giving the R, G, and B components in hexadecimals; indents indicate attributes that may be added, if desired, to the tag directly preceding it. Compatibility: HTML 3.2=part of standard HTML, up to version 3.2; *=not part of HTML 2 and probably not recognized by older browsers, N=Netscape only

Remove one indent level, button *184*

Remove one indent level, command *185*

Reply, command *117*

Reply to All, command *117*

Reply To, message part *116*

replying
    to mail *117*
    to postings *158*

resizing
    frames *38*
    panes in windows *106*

resolution, and images *193*

ROT-13
    creating *110*
    unscrambling *110*

S

Save As, command
    address books *138*
    bookmarks *87*
    browsed pages *54*
    created pages *171*

Save, command *171*

Save this Image as, command *56*

Save this Link as, command *55*

saving
    address books *138*
    addresses *131*
    bookmarks *87*
    browsed pages *54*
        without jumping *55*
    created pages *171*
        automatically *171, 254*
    images *56*
    mail password *92*
    setting autosave *254*

search services
    Altavista *64–65*
    Deja News *68*
    Excite *65*
    Lycos *65*
    Open Text *65*
    shareware.com *69*
    using Netscape to access *61*
    WhoWhere? *66–67*
    Yahoo! *62–63*

secnews.netscape.com *144*

security alerts *270*

security, and cached pages *264*

Security Preferences *269–273*
    General tab *270*
    Site Certificates tab *273*

Select All Messages, command *98*

Select Flagged Messages, command *97*

Select Thread, command *98*

selecting messages *97–98*

Send, button *115, 156*

Send, command *115*

Send Later, button *118*

Send Later, command *118, 156*

Send Mail in Outbox, command *119*

Send Now, command *156*

sending
    mail from News window *160*
    mail messages *115*
    messages in Outbox *119*
    news messages *156*

Sent folder *93*

separators
    adding *85*
    and sorting *86*
    deleting *84*

servers
    definition *23*
    setting up *260*

Servers tab, in Mail and News Preferences *112, 154, 260*

Set to Bookmark Menu Folder, command *79*

Set to New Bookmarks Folder, command *78*

shareware, finding *69*

shareware.com, search service *69*

shortcuts, creating with chain link icon *18*

Show Active Newsgroups, command *150*

Show All, command *116*

Show All Messages, command *153*

Show All Newsgroups, command *145*

Show Character Format Toolbar, command *173*

Show File/Edit Toolbar, command *173*

Show Headers, command *113*

Show Headers, submenu *155*

Show New Newsgroups, command *146*

Show Only Unread Messages, command *113, 153*

Show Paragraph Format Toolbar, command *173*

Show Subscribed Newsgroups, command *150*

signature files
    creating *129*
    specifying *261*
    using *130*

site certificates, setting up *273*

Site Certificates tab, in Security Preferences *273*

size, of images *197*

slow pages, aborting load *32*

snm files *95*

Software, command *74*

Sort Bookmarks, command *86*

Sort submenu *102, 105*

sorting
    bookmarks *86*
    messages *102*
    setting defaults *262*

sounds *41, 43*

space, adding around images *196*

spaces, adding nonbreaking *229*

Stop, button *32, 51*

Stop Loading, command *32*

stopping
    loading *32*
    text wrap *195*

Strikethrough, command *176*

strikethrough formatting *176*

subscribing to newsgroups *149*

Subscript, command *176*

Superscript, command *176*

superscripts and subscripts *176*

surfing *21–39*
    following links *24*
    frames *35–39*
    going back and forward *27*
    going back and forward in frames *39*
    going further back/ahead *28*
    going home *30*
    multimedia *44*
    reloading a page *31*
    seeing where you've been *29*
    stopping a page from loading *32*
    to FTP site *48*
    to Gopher site *49*
    to your home page *30*
    viewing images *33*
    with bookmarks *76*
    with History window *29*
    with Location field *26*
    with URL *26*

T

Table, command *214*

tables *213–226*
    adding and deleting elements *216*
    aligning cells *224*
    captions *220*
    cell height/width *223*
    changing height and width *222*
    color of *226*
    controlling line breaks *225*
    creating *213–226*
    defining border *219*
    entering text in *217*
    formatting headers *218*
    inserting new *214*
    spacing and padding cells *221*